HARDPRESS.NET
HOME OF HARD-TO-FIND BOOKS

Short Sermons
by George Frederick Prescott

Address:
HardPress
8345 NW 66TH ST #2561
MIAMI FL 33166-2626
USA
Email: info@hardpress.net

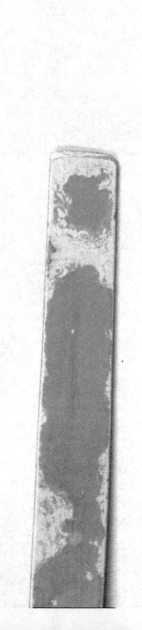

SHORT SERMONS.

BY

G. F. PRESCOTT, M. A.

INCUMBENT OF SS. MICHAEL AND ALL ANGELS,
PADDINGTON.

LONDON:

J. AND C. MOZLEY, 6, PATERNOSTER ROW;
MASTERS AND SON, 78, NEW BOND STREET.
1867.

SERMON I.

𝔐𝔦𝔠𝔥𝔞𝔢𝔩𝔪𝔞𝔰, 1866.

SPIRITUAL TEMPLES.

1 PETER, II. 5.

Ye also, as lively stones, are built up a spiritual house.

IT must have been a grand sight when Solomon's Temple was dedicated : the reverent crowd of Israelites ; the Priests and Levites in their holy vestments ; the King, fresh in his zeal for GOD, with almost priestly authority offering his fervent prayer for the Divine Blessing ; the multitude of sacrifices ; the princely festivities ; and the noble pile of buildings itself, of gigantic dimensions, with its newly-chiseled carvings, rearing its head on Mount Moriah ; and beyond all, the visible cloud by which Jehovah deigned to make His

1

Presence known and felt. There has been no such dedication service since.

But if men thought at that time, that all that beautiful apparatus for outward worship would ensure the devotion which it ought to have enkindled in the hearts of the Hebrews, they were mistaken. The Temple did not enforce piety, nor form an irresistible barrier to wickedness. In spite of GOD's Presence in that noble shrine, GOD's own people plunged on into sin; and when the LORD in Person suddenly came to His Temple, His own had no eyes to see, no heart to welcome, Him.

There is a warning in this fact which we can scarcely avoid noticing. Churches are reared up from time to time—some of them magnificent structures, worthy, so far as man's skill can ever make a building worthy, of their holy purpose;— and for this all who love GOD will be deeply thankful. But the question forces itself on our minds, Where are the ripened fruits of this pious movement for church building?

St. Peter was one of those whose eye had been caught by the magnificence of the buildings of Herod's Temple—'Master, see what manner of stones and what buildings are here!'—but he had learnt, by the time he wrote his Epistles, to set a higher value on the spiritual Temple.

There is a Temple, whose Corner-stone is Christ, whose stones are the sons of God, whose highest pinnacle is God's glory. It is an unseen building, instinct with spiritual life, for every stone is a living soul of man; and its strength and firmness consists in the union of its members, and their dependence upon Christ their sure foundation.

Solomon's Temple grew silently; the tools of the workmen were not heard, for each stone was brought ready prepared for its place. And the spiritual temple grows silently, but not less magnificently, not less securely: and if that former was glorious, much more doth this spiritual Temple exceed in glory.

The Church of the Redeemed is this Temple: the baptized are the stones of which it is composed, but they are living stones. The strength of Solomon's Temple consisted in the solid immoveability of the blocks of stone and beams of timber: the strength of the spiritual Temple lies in the stones being full of life and motion.

And each of us should learn to regard himself as a part of this spiritual Temple, built in by the Holy Spirit, to grace by his faithfulness and holiness the place where GOD delights to dwell: in other words, to let his light shine before men, that they may know him to be a Christian in very deed, by the purity, the equity, the self-sacrifice, the love, the faith, of his life; for by our fidelity and godliness shall GOD's eternal glory be best set forth.

Bear we in mind this spiritual Temple, while we turn our thoughts upon the cause of our present assembling in this House of Prayer.

Five years have passed since St. Michael's was dedicated. Since then additions have been made to its beauty, that this Temple might not be outstripped by private mansions in the costliness of its decorations. Week by week it has been filled with a greater or less gathering of worshippers. But it beseems us to enquire narrowly into the true character of those who have come hither.

St. Paul speaks apparently of the presence of angels in Christian congregations : and on the Church's Angel Festival, we may well ask ourselves, What can the angels think of us, who profess to worship GOD in this House? If they come among us, and 'hover around us while we pray,' what feelings prevail 'in the presence of the angels of GOD' as to the reality and acceptableness of our worship? Who know so well as they what true worship should be? Their harps are always in tune with living praise ; their voices are always sweet ; their hearts always pure and spiritual, for they are unfallen creatures. Upheld by eternal grace, they have not known sin, the corrupter and destroyer of holiness.

We shall not know their verdict till hereafter : but a presentiment, an instinctive consciousness of what it is, will rise in every honest mind. Oh! that we could say, 'Whatever imperfections, whatever faults or coldness, there may be in our hymns of praise, still they spring from willing and truthful hearts : we have at least had a warm desire to offer our best worship to the Almighty GOD our Saviour.'

But what does the King of angels, the all-searching Judge Himself, think of us? Does He discern a deeper tone of earnestness in us? If our Church is to be an instrument of real usefulness, it must be by becoming a rallying point of devotion, and by helping on the souls who flock into it, to a more fervent piety. Is this the result which we may trace?

There is much to encourage us : in many ways GOD has blessed the work which has been begun here. The average of congregations has not diminished; their outward behaviour is not less reverent ; and I think it may be said that the neighbourhood of the Church has grown more respectable than it was.

But with all this, it cannot be denied that fashion and curiosity have a powerful influence for attracting congregations, and men soon begin to see that it is to their own interest to conduct themselves with outward decorum.

I speak the thoughts of my colleagues, as well as my own, when I say, I am not satisfied with the result. I mark indeed some faces once scornfully averted from God's House, now thankfully turned towards it : but many more keeping

up the old course of worldly indifference, only
more hardened in sin by the constant warnings
which the church bell is ever sounding into their
ears.   And what true Christian can be satisfied,
till every heart confess to GOD, and the 'kingdoms of this world become the Kingdoms of the
LORD and of His Christ?'

There is a wide gap still to be filled up before
it can be said of St. Michael's parish and
its inhabitants as a body, 'The love of Christ
constraineth them.'   A popular book of the day *
speaks of the enthusiasm of humanity as the
distinctive mark of the Christian—ought we not
to go further, and say, that it is not only the
enthusiasm, which prompts a man to do and
suffer anything for his fellow-man, that is required
of GOD's true sons, but a spiritual enthusiasm,
which makes the love of man though a necessary
yet a subordinate part of true piety, which is
based chiefly on love of GOD.   When our souls
become, so to speak, saturated with thoughts of
GOD and Heaven, then everything on earth is
tinted with heavenly colours; work and pleasure,
and labours of lóve, spring from and are measured
by our spiritual affections; we can follow our
ordinary occupation, convinced that our work is
GOD's appointment; we can take our recreation
without forgetting His Presence, or lowering
ourselves to mere animal excitement, but as a

---

* 'Ecce Homo.'

means to recruit our minds and bodies for more devotedness to Him; and we can succour our fellow-creatures, because we see in them our dear LORD Himself stretching out His Hands for our commiseration. This is true enthusiasm: to do all for GOD, and to make His glory the central pole which attracts every one of our thoughts, words, and acts; and so to prove ourselves living stones in the spiritual Temple, and prepare, by worshipping GOD with the purity of angelic worship, to be equal unto the angels, when we shall become the children of the Resurrection.

It seems to me that the object of anniversaries is to stir up the energies which might, and generally do, flag by frequent repetition. As the hand of Eleazar, one of David's mighty men, clave to his sword through the incessant exertion of cutting down his foes, and as the oarsman's arm loses its conscious strength and springiness by long straining of the muscles, so does all energy grow faint by unintermitted employment. We need to rekindle and stir afresh our once burning thoughts, by challenging each other, and by the force and contagion of numbers, met together for the same purpose. And therefore, as St. Paul said to Timothy, let us say each to the other, 'Stir up the grace of GOD that is in thee,' and let us fling down the holy challenge to run the race of godliness, and provoke unto love and good works. Say you to us, (and may the Holy Spirit incline us to listen to your charge!) say you to us, ' " Preach the word ; be instant in season, out of season ; reprove, rebuke, exhort, with all long-suffering and doctrine ;" do the work of evangelists, and faithful pastors.' And oh! dear Brethren, listen to us, when we charge you to give yourselves up wholly to the service of GOD, remembering that of you too it is required to be faithful priests in holiness and faith, and to 'adorn the doctrine of GOD our Saviour in all things.'

These Festivals are well calculated to promote good feeling and zeal : for we meet in joy and for gratitude, and our hearts should be full, since we have great cause, as a Parish, as a Congregation, as individuals, to be grateful.

If opportunities of frequent public worship are a privilege, we have it here—you might have more services if you called for them ; if frequent Communions are prized, you have them : and whatever service we can render to you, is to the best of our powers yours to command. And if kindly feeling towards the clergy is a thing to be thankful for, we have it, I well know from my own experience. Here, then, let us join in our grateful praises to the LORD—join, because union is strength, union increases joy, efficiency, security. ' Then they that feared the LORD spake often one to another, and the LORD hearkened. . . . . . And they shall be Mine, saith the LORD of Hosts, in that day when I make up My jewels.'

May it be our blessed lot to be counted worthy of acceptance, through Christ, at the great Reckoning Day; that as we have often met together here on earth, so we may meet together hereafter in Heaven.

And if, as we know, men forget GOD because they do not see Him, and so are fettered by earthly ties, which they do see; then will the name of our Church, perpetually reminding us of the spiritual messengers of GOD, constantly recall the spiritual world, and remind us of our allegiance to the unseen GOD Himself, Who is a Spirit, LORD of men and angels.

Let us therefore go home thinking more of Heaven, more thankful for the ministry of angels, more devoted to Him Whom angels love to praise and adore.

SERMON II.

All Saints' Day.

COMMUNION OF SAINTS.

REVELATION, XIX. 14.

And the armies which were in Heaven followed Him upon white horses, clothed in fine linen, white and clean.

IF blackness and darkness convey the idea of sin and wickedness to our minds, so does whiteness that of purity and holiness. Guilt hides her head in shame, and would draw a veil over her conscious deformity. Innocence courts the light, has nothing to reserve.

When Isaiah would describe the full pardon offered to penitents, he says that sins shall be made white as snow, with every crimson stain washed out.

The essential purity of Jehovah Himself is

represented by Daniel as a garment white as snow.

Our Lord at the Transfiguration was clothed with raiment white as snow.

So were the angels at the Sepulchre.

The Priests and Levites under the Mosaic Law were arrayed in fine linen, to typify the purity which ought to reign in their souls. And it is with the like idea that the clergy of the Christian Church wear the white surplice in the celebration of divine service in Church, because every priest of Christ should be especially holy in thought, word, and deed. And whether praying therefore, or preaching, the white robe seems the most fitting and appropriate : indeed, the use of the black gown is only comparatively a modern innovation, and apparently without any sufficient reason.

Again, those who have stood by the side of an open grave will have felt, I dare say, that the clergyman's white surplice was to them a kind of bright gleam among the sad funeral shadows; to remind them that the Resurrection to eternal life, to which perhaps they hoped that their departed friend was heir, was more than a counter-balance to the sorrow of present separation ; and to symbolize the truth, that 'without holiness no man shall see the LORD,' but all is dark, dreary, painful.

Anyhow, reason and Scripture both associate white with purity.

St. John sees a vision of Christ as a triumphant conqueror. 'I saw Heaven opened, and behold! a white horse, and He that sat upon him was called Faithful and True, and in righteousness He doth judge and make war.

'His eyes were as a flame of fire, and on His Head were many crowns: and He had a Name written that no man knew but Himself.

'And He was clothed with a vesture dipped in blood: and His Name is called The WORD of GOD.

'And the armies which were in heaven followed Him upon white horses, clothed in fine linen, white and clean.'

The Captain of our salvation then is seen riding on a white horse in token of victory; and His heavenly followers ride on white horses too.

But there is a distinction. He wears a vesture dipped in blood: they are clothed in white garments. The white betokens the spotlessness of their souls, on which no stain of sin remains: for those armies are the saints or holy ones of GOD, both heavenly and human: they are the triumphant Church of the living GOD, the glorified family of the Highest.

And if Christ wears that blood-stained vesture, it is not that He is spotted or defiled with His own guilt. He is sinless, and knew sin only to vanquish it. It is His amazing love for the souls He has redeemed which makes Him wear the stains of blood upon Him, the perpetual memorial of His Cross and Passion. He is not ashamed to bear about with Him the wounds and scars of His conflict with death, which, like the soldier's dinted and battered armour, are the witnesses to His valour.

And as blood is naturally not red but white, and only reddens by contact with the impurities of the air; so Christ's blood, in which that vesture is dipped, is pure in itself and full of cleansing virtue: nay, one of the twenty-four elders told St. John that the saints had 'washed their robes and made them white in the blood of the Lamb.'

To these armies turn your thoughts on this All Saints' Day.

As the vision was prophetic, we may include among those armies the saints who have already fought the good fight, those who are now fighting, and those who hereafter shall enter into battle and conquer.

And how have these happy souls become saints beloved of GOD? The blood of the Lamb, the Son of GOD, the Son of man, has ransomed and cleansed them. It is not their own inherent virtue or courage or resolution, that has won them their blessed triumph; the brightest of these glorified spirits has no brightness of his own; all is borrowed glory, borrowed goodness, borrowed happiness. He Who died for them is the cause of it, by removing the clouds of GOD's anger, by driving out the spirit of sin from the soul, and planting in grace and holiness. They owe all to Him: by His wounds they were healed.

But what part did *they* play in the matter? What did they do towards accomplishing this happy end? Sit at ease—riot in natural excesses—continue in sin while grace was abounding? Was the work of Christ done for them, and in them, independently of them, while they were unconscious, or opposed to it? No; they recognized the hand of GOD stretched out to them, and seized hold of it; they struggled to extricate themselves. Imagine a man, whose house was being burnt over his head, when the fireman called to him to second his efforts, saying, ' No, it's your business to save me: I cannot save myself without you; I shall stay in the house, with the smoke stifling me, the rafters falling in on my head, and the cruel flames scorching me, till you come and snatch me away.' We should say that his madness deserves that he should be abandoned to his fate, though by himself alone he is totally unable to save himself.

GOD's saints are taught to help themselves. Christ will indeed deliver by His own strength alone, yet He would have them work with Him. And indeed, the struggle is hard ere they can be set safe in victory—a nature changed, a new heart, a fresh spirit, are no cheaply won laurels. And strange though it sound, long persuasions, repeated encouragements, are required before a soul can admit the presence of Christ into it. Suppose a garrison closely beset, the defence becoming each day more hopeless; the army of relief appears, and asks immediate admittance in order to continue and ensure the repulse of the besiegers; but the besieged are suspicious of their new friends, and fear a strict discipline, and refuse an entrance to their friends.

Not very different is it when man's soul will not welcome the Saviour's presence—shrinking back, and making paltry excuses, and cherishing foolish fears, which virtually show that the soul would rather perish than take any trouble to escape.

Never by indifference, never by self-indulgence, can men be made fit for heaven; but by a close earnest application to the difficulties in front of them, by resolute perseverance in avoiding sin, by faithfully resisting temptation; our soiled and torn garments can by no other means be cleansed and repaired. It is not by one single act of Christ that our spirits are once for all placed beyond the possibility of falling. Passions, corrupt inclinations, are not so to be displaced. Tribulation, sorrow, toil, patience, compose the discipline of the saints: and though many are spared outward shocks, no true saint is spared inward struggles. Those saintly white-robed armies, following the victorious Lamb of GOD in Heaven, have all passed through the contest; and

if you could look close into them, you might see
the marks of the cross which they have borne,
and they could tell of a bitter strife before they
obtained their saintly temper.

Do not you therefore, Brethren, expect without
effort and long discipline to be enrolled among the
armies of the saints.   You can know but little
of the waywardness, the reluctance, the sturdy
resistance, which your own sinful hearts raise up
against the laws of GOD, if you look to be one
day trampling down His commands, and the very
next day as resolutely obeying them.   The wild
beast is not so tamed : the raw recruit is not so
drilled into the veteran : nor is the ill-tempered,
passionate, sin-loving soul · so instantaneously
altered into the gentle simple-minded Christian.
No ; if you want to be saints, (and oh ! how we
should all glory in that title, and yearn to possess
it !) you must count upon trials and hindrances—
many a wrench of deep-rooted fancies and affections, much self-denial, frequent thwartings of
your purpose, and a path strewn with rough
stones, and hedged with sharp thorns.   But what
of that ?   No need is there to shrink from the
attempt : for if the difficulties be ever so huge,
they are not insurmountable ; and the least breath
of Heaven's atmosphere, the most imperfect entrance within those holy boundaries, is fullest
compensation for years of toil and anxious cares.
The saints toiled, some of them even unto death,

and they have gained a victory : and they beckon us on into the spiritual battle, that we may win the glorious crown too.

All Saints' Day recalls that Article of our Creed which is called 'The Communion of Saints.'

Briefly, what is meant by it? That there is a living line of union which links together all saints; issuing first from the central Throne of GOD Himself, and connecting the adorable Trinity with all created saints. There is a deep myste-rious sympathy running between all holy spiritual beings, by virtue of common tastes and common dispositions, which holds in one pleased and happy communion the Holy One Himself and His faith-ful children—the Father, the Son, the Holy Ghost, the faithful angels, the spirits of departed saints, the saints still fighting in the world. This union is broken neither by time nor distance : for as spirit is unshackled by space, so by time. And this holy fellowship is the true communion of saints. I seek not to explain more : it is only to be understood by those who stand within the mystic circle.

Now this Article of our Creed, often thought fanciful, in reality is most practical.

1. It contains a fact which is indispensable to our salvation. Communion of Saints implies the Christian's union with GOD in Christ. There is no hope for anyone unless he hold communion with Christ. 'No man cometh unto the Father,

2

but by ME.' 'Abide in ME, and I in you.' To
be a Christian at all, a man must be in close
communication with Christ our LORD—must
learn His temper, trust in His merits, lean on
His power, follow His steps : must be a very
member, a very limb, of the Body of Jesus Christ:
the same spiritual blood must run through his
veins, the same holy life must live in him, which
lives in Christ.   And therefore to believe in the
communion with saints is necessary, for our salvation depends on our communion with Christ,
the Chief of Saints.

2. The thought that we may hold communion
with the saints is encouraging : we are reminded
of their triumph, and incited to emulate their
exertions ; we may feel that they watch us, take
a lively interest in us, rejoice over our faithfulness. Pray to them we may not, for we are
bidden to seek succour only from Christ ; nor
indeed do we know whether, if we did pray to
them, they could hear us ; and prayer to them
would soon insensibly slide into worship.   But
still it is a source of strength to think of them.
Everyone knows the power of sympathy.   It is
inspiriting to feel that there are others, even
though personally unknown, or unseen, who care
for the same things which we care for.   It is a
real pleasure, and not mere fancy, that other
beings are praising the same Master Whom we
praise, and have been already saved, by the same

Saviour, by Whom we hope ourselves to be saved.

And is there not pleasure in cherishing the thought of a secret intercourse between us and the spirits of our friends who have been called out of this world? To know that death, though it rend the bodily union between us, cannot sever the spiritual links, is very soothing in time of bereavement. The mother laying her child in the grave, whom she has watched growing up with more than earthly sanctity or innocence, can stay on David's words, ' I shall go to him, but he shall not return to me.' The man who closes the eyes of a friend, whose soul has been one with his own life, is conscious that it is only a half parting: the closed eyes are still beaming on his inward mind, the cord of sympathy is not snapt. 'Tis but a few years, and in person again they will be re-united in GOD'S presence. Surely such an one can rejoice to believe in the Communion of Saints.

3. Again, by remembering that the saints, who have passed from this scene of sin and sorrow, may be aware of and mourn over our faults, we shall be reproved and put to shame in our consciences. Not unfrequently the question rises to a man's heart in a moment of temptation, What would my mother have said had she been still living? How could I look my dear friend in the face, if he were still before me? And such a thought seems to show that the questioner believes

in some sort of intercourse subsisting between this world and the saints who have gone to their rest. If so, it has its benefit, for it may deter from sin. You may call it a low motive; but if a hatred of sin be stirred by even a lower motive, do not quench the motive, and so leave the sin unchecked.

Oh! be we all fired with noble rivalry by that vision of the pure and victorious armies of the saints! They should be to us but the vanguard of the host, and we should strive and pray that we may be enabled to follow them into the combat, and having fought the good fight, to stand with them in triumph. Why should not we be arrayed as an army of saints on earth? Some are ashamed to fight under such a motto. What! ashamed of being brothers and sisters of the holy and good in olden times? ashamed of being partners with those, who out of love for Christ laid down their lives? ashamed of walking hand in hand with Abraham, Samuel, St. John, and St. Paul? ashamed of being like the angels in Heaven? Nay, let us take shame to be with sinners, to fear the world's reproaches; but never be ashamed of all that is true, and noble, and saintly.

May the Spirit of the Holy One make us all saints; that, living after the likeness of Him Who knew no sin, we may hereafter be like Him, pure and victorious.

SERMON III.

Whitsunday.

THE HOLY SPIRIT.

ACTS, II. 4.

And they were all filled with the Holy Ghost.

How can men ever bring themselves to doubt that there is a spiritual invisible world? How, with all the proofs of an invisible self, can a man believe that what we see with our bodily eyes is all that exists for us? Does not everyone feel that he has a living something within him, a moving conscious thing, part of himself, inseparable from himself, although out of sight? Call it what you will—mind, soul, spirit—there it is: you cannot cease to have it, without ceasing to live.

And around this spirit of man cling many unholy parasites, so to speak; thoughts that will not bear the light, affection for sin, coldness towards GOD, indifference to all that is not part of this scene of our mortal life—thoughts which we cannot shake off without some aid, which it lies not with ourselves to furnish.

To reach these inward corruptions, there is wanted an influence different from those outside forces which are brought to bear on ordinary things in this world—a spiritual influence—and this, not some subtle power of mere matter, working like a potent drug on the animal frame, or like an electric battery, lifeless with all its force ; but a personal intelligent influence, acting with wisdom and kindness.

Nothing short of a *person* will do.   Books, laws, circumstances, have a power of persuasion ; but that is not enough, for each case has its own peculiarities, and needs separate treatment.   We might as well talk of a thinking machine, as suppose that when there are spiritual faculties to address, any but a spirit—that is, an invisible person, can penetrate to the point requiring to be reached.

Such a Person is the Holy Spirit, in Whose special honour we keep this Whitsunday.

The Holy Scriptures plainly describe Him as a Person :—' The Holy Ghost *said,* Separate ME Barnabas and Saul.'   ' *Grieve* not the Holy Spirit of GOD.'   ' The Spirit Itself *maketh intercession* for us.'   ' He will *guide* you into all truth.'

Such texts at once claim for Him all those sensibilities which ought to excite our regard and confidence, and convince us that what He does is done not under any irresistible destiny, but of His own free Will, of Love, not of tyranny and oppressiveness.

Again, this is no disparagement of the work of Christ. He is the only Atonement, the One Mediator; none cometh unto the Father but by Him. Yet He Himself said, ' It is expedient for you that I go away; for if I go not away, the Comforter will not come unto you.' Expedient, because His local bodily Presence would be exchanged for the universal Presence of the Spirit, Who would bring His influence to bear on every spirit of man in every place. Christ came into the world to execute a certain act, by sacrificing Himself, and to lay out before us a certain example and model of what is required of us. This done, He departed : ' It was finished.' He had shown matchless love and unselfishness, had conciliated GOD, had thrown open the gates of Heaven, and having completed His work on earth, ascended to carry on the heavenly part of His high office—intercession for man, which shall employ Him for ever, till the world ends. And His place on earth is taken by the Blessed Spirit, the Comforter—the Source of strength, consolation, spiritual life—to abide with us for ever—for ever, while life lasts; for ever, while temptations press; for ever, while sin besets; for ever, while Satan is unbound, and not chained in the bottomless pit.　There is no need to sorrow, as the disciples did because the LORD was going from them, at the thought that the Spirit may leave us, so long as we desire His Presence : only will obstinate relentless hatred of His work make Him sadly ' take His everlasting flight.'

Our blessed LORD had said, ' I will pray the Father, and He shall send you another Comforter, that He may abide with you for ever;' and on the Feast of Pentecost after His Ascension, the Comforter came down upon the little flock gathered in prayer, waiting for the promise.

Once again, GOD, Who had compassionated man's infirmity, and sent His Son in human form that man might trust and believe Him, studied our weakness by vouchsafing a visible token of the Spirit's Presence.　There was a rush of mighty wind filling the house, and separate flames of fire sat on each head, significant emblems of the power of the Holy Ghost, penetrating as air, overpowering as wind, purifying as fire, breathing warmth and life into the soul.

He came to the disciples so.　He filled them with Himself, quickened their zeal, their spiritual perceptions, their love for Christ, their trust in His merits, their devotion to His service.　From that hour the little company went forth, divinely led, divinely harnessed, divinely strengthened, divinely nourished by secret communion with their ascended LORD.　The Comforter had come ;

all the promise had been more than realized. They felt, as never before, that the spirit world was a reality, and that they had an intimate concern with it; and possessed with this thought, they went forth to win souls to GOD. Oh! that all pastors and missionaries now might assay their work in a kindred spirit! Oh! that all those who next Sunday shall have the hands of a Bishop laid on their heads, may in like manner be filled with the Holy Ghost, and the Church of our LORD receive a strong accession of faithful men eager in the strength of GOD to do battle with the enemies of the Cross.

Brethren, did the Holy Ghost on that Pentecost only come down for that generation? Has He gone back to the Father and the Son? Well He might have done so; for subsequent generations have done all they could to grieve Him and drive Him back. But no: He came to abide for ever, till the end comes; with all His gentle long-suffering watching for opportunities, ready, though an unwelcome guest too often, to wait till some souls should take Him in and cherish Him.

The gift was to us, as well as to those one hundred and twenty who met in the upper chamber. The Presence of the Holy Ghost is as certain, though no mighty wind, no earthquake, no fire, accompany His approach; for the still small Voice does come and make Itself heard too.

Many times, many ways, He comes. He comes

at our Baptism, when we are 'born again of water
and of the Spirit.' He comes at our Confirm-
ation, when by the laying on of hands the
blessing of the Holy Ghost is conveyed to the
faithful seeker for it. He comes at the Holy
Table, when we strive to feed on Christ; and if
the Holy Ghost be not there, we cannot; for
faith, which we then need, is GOD's gift, and all
good and perfect gifts the Spirit brings down
for us. He comes hovering secretly round us,
when we pore over the pages of that Book which
He has filled with His own Truth : and you
cannot read the Bible honestly, without being
fanned by the wings of the Holy Dove, Who
points the moral of every Scripture story, and
brings home to the conscience every Scripture
precept. He comes 'in visions of the night,
when deep sleep falleth on man,' or when you lie
awake in thought and communing with your own
spirit; He presents Himself to your inward sen-
sations, and what you think of good is His
suggestion. He comes—sometimes with a stern
look, in sorrows and trials; and by a holy discipline
He ingratiates Himself with the soul, and opens
a way into the heart ; and there He sets up
before your mind the image of Christ crucified,
and bids it conform itself to those sufferings. He
comes—sometimes with joy and peace, when the
soul has learnt to fling off all self-trust and
independence as well as all aversion to divine

things ; and then He pours in His Presence,
filling the soul with a flood of holy comfort, that
lifts a man out of himself, and makes him in-
sensible to all the changes and chances of this
mortal life. And when so He comes, He brings
an earnest of that eternal bliss, for which all His
influence is designed to prepare us.

Who, then, will shrink from asking himself,
' Have I the Spirit in my heart, and do I love to
let Him have free course within me, and mould
my every wish after His own holy Will ? '

Should it be difficult to discern whether or not
He is in us? For when He is settled in us, He
will fill us. There will be a true enthusiasm ;
not like that of the priestess of Apollo at Delphi
in the times of Greek idolatry—a frenzy of uncontrollable excitement, a very possession of mind
and body—but a quiet yet penetrating influence,
stealing into every corner of the heart, touching,
warming, sanctifying, every disposition ; thrusting
out, not with mad violence, but by an irresistible
majestic advance, every thought of wickedness,
every longing for unspiritual pleasures, making
the heart the dwelling-place of all ' love, joy,
peace, long-suffering, gentleness, goodness, faith,
meekness, temperance.' If He is in us, we cannot
be passionate, intemperate, selfish, sensual ; but
must be aiming at GOD's glory, loving Christ our
Saviour, and living with Christ in spirit, hoping
for actual life with Christ hereafter.

Brethren, you can all answer these questions for yourselves. In GOD's name, do answer them. And if they cannot bear to be answered, think how the Holy Spirit grieves that His patient loving inspirations are in vain, and that He cannot make you love the Saviour, Who loved you unto the death. But if the answer is such that you can thank GOD for it, oh! cherish the Sacred Guest within you, that His fulness may abide in you, and that you may ' increase in this Holy Spirit more and more, until you come to His everlasting kingdom.'

SERMON IV.

Trinity.

THE TRINITY.

ISAIAH, VI. 3.

Holy, Holy, Holy, is the LORD *of hosts.*

UZZIAH (or Azariah, 2 Kings, xv. 7.) was a living monument of the danger of intruding into sacred things beyond what is permitted. He had presumed, in the pride of feeling himself monarch at Jerusalem, to enter the Temple and burn incense, an office exclusively assigned to the consecrated sons of Aaron. Azariah, the High Priest, with fourscore priests, boldly followed and remonstrated with him; and as Uzziah stood, censer in hand, boiling with rage at this interference with his will, the LORD struck him, and on the instant the priests saw the plague-spot of leprosy rise on his forehead. Forthwith 'they thrust him out from thence;

yea, himself hasted to go out.' And thenceforth he was debarred from ever entering the Holy Precincts, in which he had sacrilegiously thought to reign supreme. He was a leper to the day of his death—a marked man, and 'dwelt in a several house.'

It seems almost by way of contrast with this, that the prophet Isaiah describes the vision which was vouchsafed to him, unasked, in the year that King Uzziah died; while he himself, the very reverse of the presumptuous king, is penetrated with a deep awe and trembling, because, though not by his own seeking, he had become a witness of the Glory of GOD. 'Woe is me! . . . . for mine eyes have seen the King, the LORD of Hosts.'

The prophet expresses the true feelings which ought to rise in man's heart from the contemplation of the Divine Majesty; and this seems a suitable subject for Trinity Sunday.

Our loving guide, the Church, has led us round the whole cycle of Christian doctrine, making the prominent incidents in our LORD's Life to act as landmarks to shew the track of the Truth. Advent rouses a consciousness of sin, and of our miserable condition by nature, stirs up repentance, and bids the heart prepare to meet its GOD. Christmas heralds in the Birth of the Saviour, and points to the new birth of man's soul, which is to change us from children of wrath to children of grace. Lent leads us on through the sufferings of the LORD, coming to their height on the Cross on Good Friday, to gaze on the Death which purchased life for us. Easter kindles the flame of hope, in the prospect of the Resurrection, without which the soul has no anchor. Ascension Day shews us the work carried on in Heaven. Whitsunday commemorates the arrival of that living Power, Who by His holy influence is to perfect and strengthen the life which we are to live in Christ. And now on Trinity Sunday we gather up the lessons of all this teaching, and dwell on the magnitude of GOD's Love, streaming down to us in a threefold channel, by Creation, Redemption, and Sanctification.

The grand doctrine of to-day is the Trinity in Unity, viz., that in the One GOD there exist Three Persons.

Proof of this we draw not from philosophic argument, but from Holy Scripture, that is, from GOD's own Revelation of Himself.

1. GOD is *One*. 'Hear, O Israel: the LORD thy GOD is one LORD.' 'Thou believest that there is one GOD; thou doest well.' 'Thou shalt have none other Gods but Me.' These, with countless other passages, imply and establish the unity of GOD.

But 2. *Three* several persons are mentioned—the Father, the Son, the Spirit.

(a.) 'My *Father*, of whom ye say that He is
          your GOD.'
      'One GOD and *Father* of all.'
      'Our fellowship is with the *Father*.'
      'To the glory of GOD the *Father*.'
      'Your *Father*, which is in Heaven.'

(b.) 'Of the *Son* He saith, Thy throne, O
          GOD.'
      'The *Word* was GOD.'
      'As the Father hath life in Himself, so
          hath He given the *Son* to have life
          in Himself.'
      'Declared to be the *Son* of GOD with
          power.'
      'We know that the *Son* of GOD is come.'

(c.) 'No man knoweth the things of GOD,
          but the *Spirit* of GOD.'
      'Why hath Satan filled thine heart to
          lie to the *Holy Ghost?* .... thou hast
          not lied unto men, but unto GOD.'
      'Ye are the temple of GOD .... your bodies
          are temples of the *Holy Ghost*.'

All these are evidently distinct separate
Persons. The Father sends the Son, the Son
comes from the Father, the Holy Ghost proceeds
from the Father and the Son. Note, however,
that Person in this case is not equivalent to
'person' in the common sense, which implies a
separate existence. In the GODhead, the Three
Persons compose One GOD; in human nature,

three persons can in no sense be called one man.

How are we to accept this mysterious doctrine?

1. It is reasonable that GOD's nature should be incomprehensible. It is admitted that the nature of the Creator must be different from that of the creature—must be transcendently superior. But even our own nature we do not understand—our triple nature, body, soul, and spirit? How does our life go on? What is the primary motive power in our lungs? Explain this, before you ask an explanation of the Divine Nature.

Again, there are other beings, animals or spirits, whose existence is a riddle to us. We believe angels to be spirits, but understand not what is meant by spirits.

One another we cannot decipher; there is so great a variety of feelings, tastes, pursuits, minds: we are content with saying, 'Men are not alike, and therefore we do not understand others.' Certainly this is a reason for not understanding each other; but the mystery remains unsolved, how and why we are not all alike.

Is it then to be expected that He Whom we call GOD should be such an one as we can bring down to the level of our comprehension?

Some who deny the doctrine of the Trinity, because inexplicable, hold that GOD is everywhere; is that to be explained?

The truth is, we must receive many things as

3

mysteries, beyond the capacity of our understanding. It is far better to face the question
generally, and admit the principle. Either we
must claim the right to reduce all things to
our own intelligence, or we must submit to feel
that some things are above it; and I do not
see how we are to hold truth at all, unless we
are prepared to believe in some things which
stagger our minds. That man must have little
wisdom, who can think himself so wise as to
have nothing to learn; and if we have much
to learn one from another, it is monstrous to
suppose that we have nothing to learn from
GOD, Who is in a sphere transcendently above
our limited sphere.

Whatever other argument might be adduced
to disprove the doctrine of the Trinity in
Unity, this argument, drawn from its being
inconceivable, is of no value at all, for it might
be used equally against the fact that the acorn
grows into the oak, against the power of moral
influence, against the distances of the heavenly
bodies from each other, against the existence
of electricity.

To find, therefore, GOD'S Nature described
in terms which convey no idea to our minds,
so far from making us incredulous, should be
a reason for listening attentively, because it
would be irrational to expect a description
which was intelligible.

Whether practice, or our future elevation to a higher sphere, with higher capacities, will ever enable us to possess more insight into this mystery, is one thing; but quite another, that our first lesson in knowledge should give us a full and complete grasp of the truth. Here it must be, 'line upon line, precept upon precept.'

Be it also remembered, that we can know nothing concerning GOD, but what He chooses to disclose; and if we are staggered by His disclosure, we have no ground for doubting it. Back, over-curious reason! Back, presumptuous searching! and let us never forget that the doctrine of the Trinity is disclosed to us by GOD Himself, and that it is not contrary to, but only above, human reason!

Let the sceptic, and those who pride themselves on rejecting all that does not fall in with their preconceived and narrow notions, cavil at this mystery, which the Church has always held. Let us take the more reasonable course, of asking whether it is borne out by Holy Scripture; and when we find that it is, let us receive it as irrefragable, and honestly and patiently cherish it.

In Isaiah's vision there is much that is instructive.

The Seraphic hymn contains apparently an allusion to the mystery of the threefold GOD-head: 'Holy, Holy, Holy,' thrice repeated.

But even if that interpretation cannot be sustained, still the repetition would give force and solemnity to the expression, used at the same time with a description of the wondrous glories which surrounded the throne of the Almighty. Like Moses at the burning bush, afraid to look upon GOD, so the holy Prophet Isaiah trembled at the sight of that dazzling glory. And if we know more of the Divine Nature, more distinctly revealed to us in the Gospel, all the more need for us to stand in awe.

And men need this lesson. Little, indeed, do the most solemn and awful verities abash the minds of some people. Men who can take GOD's hallowed Name in vain—can pass their ribald senseless jests on the language of Holy Scripture, or on the solemn truths sacred to the Saints—do need to be checked, and convinced of the guilt of their course, and of the peril of rousing a Power, which can in an instant crush them down into unceasing tortures. These awful doctrines are not things to play with, or whet the edge of our cleverness upon. If GOD has revealed anything of His Nature, it is rather that, by what He does reveal, He may repress further curiosity, by shewing how hopeless a task it is to try to fathom the depths of His Nature.

And it is no wonder that His Temple is often

desecrated by careless or unholy behaviour, when we feel no reverence for the Divine Being Himself. Do men dare think, forsooth, that He has the imperfections and infirmities of some earthly monarch? or at least, will wink at the thoughtless irreverence of poor weak man? He Himself forbid it, that we should harbour a thought so foolish, so blasphemous! Stand in awe, all of you, Brethren and Sisters, and sin not. Stand in awe, 'for our GOD is a consuming fire.' And as, if every ray of light were excluded, and you felt deep darkness wrapping itself round you, you would grope your way, and hold your breath, lest haply some accident might overtake you, and you might injure yourself in the darkness; so, as you look upon the mystery of GOD, tread softly and warily; keep your senses on the stretch; be careful with an absorbing care. Measure the distance between Him and you— Him in Heaven, you on earth; and whether studying His written Word, be humble, and fear; whether offering worship, tremble lest you should worship amiss; whether looking for His Presence and Influence in the events of your life, watch soberly, and pray that you may be obedient to His teaching; and that, whatever His Will declare, you may receive it with unquestioning submission.

But mark these Seraphim. Their wings they partly use to screen their eyes from the dazzling glare of that unapproachable Light, but partly for action. 'With twain they covered their face, with twain they covered their feet, and with twain they did fly.' Therefore, while bending our eyes to the ground, while not seeking to let the world see how we are-walking, we should still never let our wings tire in the work which GOD gives us to do. Adoration means not indolence; worship is not idleness; but we adore that we may be diligent; we worship that we may all the more faithfully serve.

A king's servant does obeisance, listening attentively to hear how he may do his sovereign's behest. The Christian will best shew his fidelity by active devotion to the part given him to do. A man all day on his knees—if ever such an one could be found in this cold though restless age—would but prove his want of wisdom, and his little sense of what GOD loves us to do. 'Be faithful unto death,' is a charge which implies wearing ourselves out for GOD, braving dangers for GOD, submitting to agonies for GOD, renouncing self, tastes, prejudice, everything, to keep up the spiritual life, by becoming dead to all that is unspiritual. Fly with untired wings; move swiftly in the course which Christ lays down; make the most of your brief time, but temper your speed with awe; strengthen your awe with vigorous action.

Harness together faith and works. Be humble, yet active; and so be like the Seraphim, meet to sing the Trisagion, 'Holy, Holy, Holy,' with angels hereafter.

But though the doctrine of the Trinity is above us, we may find practical benefit in believing it. 'A threefold cord is not quickly broken.' In the Work of our Salvation, we have a threefold almightiness, Three perfect Friends, Each exercising a Divine influence, yet Each acting in truest concert with the Others. For They are Friends indeed, All capable of severity when needed, but All overflowing with Love. See how unitedly They work. The Father is a jealous GOD; The Lamb has wrath hereafter; The Spirit is grieved, perhaps. Yet are All tender towards us, All actively and unweariedly engaged in providing blessings for poor fallen man.

It is difficult even to speak of things infinite; and it might be said that any One of the Three Persons is fully able to complete and execute the whole Work of Redemption. We do not deny it. But still, completed and executed as it is by Three separate Persons, it seems to have a more life-like power in it. If there was a bare 'fiat' issued, 'Let man be saved,' we, in our weakness and infatuation, might disbelieve the intention and efficacy of the command. But this we cannot do, when - we are told of the

Father not sparing the Son, but freely giving Him up for us all; of the Son submitting to a life of suffering and tortures to come among us and succour us; and of the Holy Ghost maintaining a constant work in our hearts. We are forced to discern in this a deep compassion, which touches the heart, and stirs up good hope. And the Love of GOD, thus in three ways manifested, constrains us, and fills us with fresh gratitude.

Brethren, we cannot spare the doctrine of the Trinity. Deny it, and you cut away from under our feet all the foundation of our faith. The Oneness of GOD is a grand fact, but not contradicted by the Threefoldness of GOD. The Love of the Father is ineffable; but surely, our adoration and love must be increased by the remembrance of all· the sympathies which the Son has purchased by His Incarnation, and of all the intercessions of the Spirit, our Guide and Comforter.

Men think to simplify religion by denying this doctrine; but without it the Power of GOD's Love is diluted, and borders on a cold mechanical tyranny, without the warmth of infinite pity, and manifold sensibilities.

So too, I think, the sense of Home in Heaven, of the Father's House, of its many mansions, of the Heavenly Family, fades away when we forget the Three Persons, revives when we recollect the Three Persons. If the threefold Help will bring us more easily to Heaven, the threefold Presence will be more life to us there; joy in every form and shape; the relationships of father, brother, friend, each in its fulness, all in a blessed union.

In your struggles with your three enemies, world, flesh, devil, the Three Friends are with you; they will be your champions here, and hereafter your exceeding great reward.

SERMON V.

REGENERATION.

St. John, iii. 5.

Verily, verily, I say unto thee, Except a man be born of water and of the Spirit, he cannot enter into the Kingdom of God.

How little we know our own hearts, or our soul's necessities! Nicodemus had probably lived for years under the notion that he was walking in the right path, and knew the Truth. Doubtless he had studied the Old Testament prophecies, and was expecting the Messiah; but having read them with a somewhat prejudiced eye, he had only half understood them. Jacob's prophecy of 'Shiloh,' Isaiah's of the 'Wonderful, Counsellor, the Mighty God,' were familiar; but others equally true and important he overlooked, apparently: the sufferings and pain with which the 'Man of Sorrows' was to be crowned, he had not realized.

He was a man with burning thoughts and earnest longings, and could not help being struck with the miracles which Jesus was working. Yet to have gone to Him openly to ask His counsel would have been a step too galling to his pride, and inconsistent with his prudence : and so he comes by night.

Very gentle is GOD's dealing with those who are timid. Weak faith is encouraged, and led on, till it gathers strength by exercise. And Nicodemus from coming by night advanced to speaking openly before the Sanhedrim, and later on, to boldly joining in the Burial of the LORD.

But it must have cost him a great effort to come at all. He, 'The Master of Israel,' the popular Professor of the day, the guide of the blind, the teacher of babes, on whose advice numbers were hanging—he, to come as a learner ! The high Pharisee to sit at the feet of the obscure carpenter !

It was a knowledge of this inward struggle that in part disposed Christ to receive him so tenderly.

But at once He shows him that all his ideas on the nature of Messiah's kingdom were erroneous. Peace, freedom at home, conquest abroad—Israel exalted, the Gentiles at Israel's feet—the Law of Moses the law of the world—the Passover the grand Feast for every race—the reign of Solomon, with all its grandeur, wealth, and dignity, revived in increased glory, by a greater than Solomon. This was Nicodemus's dream—a false view.

'You look to see the Kingdom of GOD? It is a spiritual Kingdom. Those who would see must have spiritual sight. "Except a man be born again, (or 'from above,') he cannot see the Kingdom of GOD."'

Nicodemus understood it not. 'Born again! who ever heard of man being twice born? Born, when a man is old, as I am! How can a man be born again when he is old?'

Yet the spiritual Kingdom could have no real existence to those who could not see spiritually. Abraham had rejoiced to see Messiah's day, and he saw it and was glad—saw it by spiritual faith. Elisha was calm when his foes had encompassed the city to take him, because he could see, by an inward sight, the mountains full of chariots of fire and horses of fire round about him. Such a sight of faith Nicodemus had not, but needed—he could only see with his outward eyes.

Our LORD explains further. 'Except a man be born of water and of the Spirit, he cannot enter into the Kingdom of GOD.' If men are to be citizens of this inward Kingdom, they must have an inward qualification for it : just as they are born with bodies of flesh for living on the earth, so must they be born with spiritual faculties and emotions for taking part in the invisible Kingdom of GOD.

This remarkable text implies the necessity of our being born of water and of the Spirit before we can be citizens of the Kingdom of GOD—the spiritual Kingdom, which, commencing on earth, is to be unfolded for our full and unalloyed enjoyment in Heaven.

It is a true rule for the interpretation of Holy Scripture, to take the literal sense where it is possible. This text has been explained by some to be merely a figurative expression, implying that there must be a complete change of heart, and that the spirit of a man must be entirely cleansed from sin, just as water cleanses outward things, and this by the work of the Holy Spirit. This seems very forced, for there is no metaphor— 'washed,' had that word been used, might have been : nor is there a simile, for no word of comparison is employed.

The universal interpretation put upon this text by the old Fathers was that the allusion in the word 'water' was to Holy Baptism. And it is hard to see any difficulty in this explanation.

We know that St. John the Baptist had introduced a Baptism by water : numbers availed themselves of it : Jesus Himself submitted to it, and so sanctioned it.

St. Luke tells us that the Pharisees and Lawyers rejected the counsel of GOD against themselves, being not baptized of him. The Pharisee Nicodemus therefore had probably rejected it. Yet if this kept him from believing in St. John's mission, it was strange, because Baptism was a common ceremony for initiating proselytes into the Jewish Church.

Christ's mission went beyond St. John's. 'I indeed baptize with water unto repentance; He shall baptize you with the Holy Ghost and with fire.' And this completion of Baptism took place at Pentecost, when the disciples were bathed with tongues of fire, and filled with the Holy Ghost. It is also remarkable that the conversation with Nicodemus is followed immediately by an account of Jesus (*i.e.* His disciples) baptizing.

'Born of water and of the Spirit.' Therefore the water of Baptism and the grace of the Spirit are needed to produce the New Birth. Christ unites them, we cannot separate them. Those baptized (if only the Baptism be a proper and valid Baptism) are born again of water and of the Spirit.

Several other passages confirm this view.

'The washing of regeneration and renewing of the Holy Ghost.'

'The like figure whereunto, even Baptism, doth also now save us. . . .'

'He that believeth and is baptized shall be saved.'

'Repent and be baptized every one of you for the remission of sins.'

'As many of you as have been baptized into Christ, have put on Christ.'

These texts connect the New Birth with Baptism. And that this is the view of the Church of England is shewn, (1) By the introduction of my text into the Office for the Baptism of Adults, as proving the necessity of Baptism : (2) By the declaration made after the washing by water in the Office for Infant Baptism, 'Seeing now that this Infant *is* regenerate.'

Look at Baptism honestly, and see what is done for you there ; a marvellous spiritual change takes place—a change of our relation to GOD spiritually.

An objection is raised : 'It is unintelligible that water should be connected with an inner change.' The same might be alleged against the use of bread and wine in the LORD'S Supper. And it is not said that water alone produces the spiritual effect, but water with the Spirit. But grant it unintelligible, still our obedience to GOD'S Will must not be regulated by our understanding the reason of it. This was how Eve fell. 'I do not see why I should not eat of fruit so good and evidently desirable.' It is enough, on this point, if the LORD says, 'Except a man . . . .' Another objection is, that we see converts, holy and evidently changed men, yet unbaptized. But this is not to the purpose. The world would have said that Nicodemus was good, and needed certainly no radical change. Yet to him it is that our LORD pointedly says, 'Except

a man be born of water and of the Spirit, he
cannot enter . . .' And the argument would be
tenable, I suppose, that if such men had been
baptized they would have been much better men.
And we are speaking not of exceptional cases,
but of the ordinary channel of the flow of GOD'S
grace.

Men speak of Baptism as an ecclesiastical fancy,
a mere whim of man ; forgetting how our Saviour
designates it. If He instituted it, commanded it,
made it essential, I see not how it can be called a
human fancy to obey His command, to exalt His
Institution, to press the necessity of receiving it.

After all, the objectors to Holy Baptism are—

(1.) Men purely irreligious, who have no ap-
preciation of anything spiritual. These it is
impossible to convince, till they are first convinced of the existence and importance of spiritual
things. Of course, if a man does not believe in
the Kingdom of GOD, he can have no capacity
for understanding the manner of introduction
into that spiritual Kingdom. To him naturally
Baptism appears merely the sprinkling of a few
drops of water, with certain cabalistic or magic
words ; and he pities the poor creatures who are
the dupes of such imposture. Be it so ! He
might say the same of every spiritual exercise, of
the very idea of worship at all.

Or (2.) those whose eyes are riveted on the
immediate operation of the Spirit, and who forget

that all the operations of that Holy One are
addressed to men who live in an outer world,
surrounded by things of sense, to be touched or
seen—to men who have bodies and emotions as
well as a spiritual being. That water and the
Spirit should really be associated seems to them
incredible; and therefore, out of fancied respect
for the living Agent, the Holy Spirit, they assert
the uselessness of the formal part of Baptism, viz.,
the water.

Yet the connection of outer and inner things
is not so uncommon. A look touches on and
penetrates the heart: a word awakens emotion :
a sermon rouses perhaps, where the mind would
have continued dead had the preacher's voice
been silent; and it seems to me that the difficulty
would be far greater in believing in spiritual
operations unconnected with outward things.

Perhaps the truth is this. There is a strong
dislike among some to doctrines which involve
passive faith. Some will accept only those
spiritual truths which seem to be approached by
a spiritual struggle, felt and active. In prayer
and study of Holy Scripture they find room for
an active exercise of their own powers. It is the
old error of trying to procure our own salvation
by our own exertions. The idea of prayer is of a
struggle in which indomitable persistency will
ensure conquest to the struggler. But we are to
be saved by faith, and faith must be in such

4

matters passive. Noah's faith consisted in a passive long-sustained belief in the simple word of GOD, accompanied indeed - by work, trying work, in the face of great ridicule, but itself a belief that rose calmly above all questionings, all clamours of reason. As the trial then was, 'Build, and thou shalt be saved in and by water;' so in Baptism the trial is, 'Wash, and the Spirit shall cleanse thy soul.'

Our text, then, declares water and the Spirit to be essential requisites for bringing about the New Birth. Applying this to the two cases, we find :—(1) As to Infant Baptism. The water is there, and the Spirit we believe to be there too, because there is nothing in the unconscious child to hinder the presence of the Holy Spirit, Who loves to deal with the guileless heart in which is no conscious wickedness. (2) As to Adult Baptism. The water is there, but whether the Spirit is there depends on the preparation of the heart. 'If thou believest with all thy heart, thou mayest.' If there is no faith, there is no valid Baptism. Hence we conclude that Infant Baptism is always accompanied by the New Birth, Adult Baptism only when accompanied by faith.

If, then, you were baptized in riper years, look well into the ground of your security. If the motive was not simple faith then, pray for the gift of faith now, that your former Baptism by water may be supplemented by spiritual Baptism now.

But most of you were baptized in infancy. You were then born again. Whether you are cowardly soldiers, unfaithful subjects, unfruitful branches, unanswering to the heavenly gifts which descended on you, is quite another question. Once in the Church, once in the Bosom of Christ, once having seen and entered into the Kingdom of GOD, is not the same as being finally saved. The prodigal had his portion of goods, and squandered all: Solomon had the special gift of wisdom, and lost it: Judas had the bag, but it ruined his soul: the Jews had the oracles of GOD, but crucified their King. You have had the New Birth given you, (it is a gift, not an acquisition,) the seed is in you : with some, growing, shooting forth, blossoming, bearing fruit— oh! may yours be a rich harvest!—with some, drooping, scarcely out of the ground, or perhaps hidden altogether—yet it is there. Oh! pray for rain and sun to quicken it: feel for it, as the blind would: grasp it, cherish it, feed on it! And though you have never yet felt it, you shall feel it: though men never have seen it, they shall see it. Stir up the gift of GOD that is in you. You are His children, His heirs; come forward, and live as conscious inheritors of the Kingdom of Heaven.

SERMON VI.

EUCHARIST.
Sunday before Easter.

St. John, vi. 53.

Verily, verily, I say unto you, Except ye eat the Flesh of the Son of Man, and drink His Blood, ye have no life in you.

The immediate effect of these words, spoken in the synagogue at Capernaum, was that many of the disciples said, 'This is an hard saying; who can hear it?'—an offensive saying to their stubborn prejudices.

Shall it be to us a hard saying? Shall we 'go back, and walk no more with Him?'

The words have a double meaning.

1. A short time before, our Blessed Lord had fed five thousand men in the desert with bread and fish. Having dismissed the multitude, He crossed the sea. The people, hastily crossing

the water, followed Him, and found Him at Capernaum. He tells them plainly that He knew why they came after Him; not for instruction, to learn Truth, or out of reverence for Him, but selfishly: 'Ye seek Me, not because ye saw the miracles, but because ye did eat of the loaves, and were filled.' And then He exhorts them to choose a higher aim: 'Labour not for the meat which perisheth, but for that meat which endureth unto everlasting life.' And so He tells them of the true Bread, which is Himself, the Life and strength of the soul.

Now in this Discourse the first meaning is, that Christ coming into the world as Incarnate GOD is the source of man's salvation, and that, to receive the benefits of His coming, we must believe in Him. We must come to Him for our soul's safety, hang our trust on His merits, strengthen our spirits with a strong yearning for Him. We must have Him abiding in us, the life of our souls; His Power must transform our spirits; closer than the limpet clings to the rock, must man cling to Christ; more needful than meat and drink to our bodies is He, the All-nourishing, needful to our souls. As a starved and famished frame cannot stand up, in its tottering faintness, against the wear and weight of labour; so man cannot make head against Satan without the Divine Saviour dwell-

ing in him, nor stand before the Judgment-seat
of GOD, unless the GOD-Man stands by, and
holds his hand, and whispers comfort, and pleads
his cause. Yes, we die—spiritually die—without
Christ; for no subtilty of ours can exculpate
us, no boldness of ours can face eternal wrath,
no purity of ours can produce singleness of
mind towards GOD. There is no remnant of
hope by which, unaided, we can rest on His
Love. Christ must do and be all for us—
our Light, our Confidence, our Redeemer from
iniquity, our Hope—Christ must be our Life, our
Food.

2. But the text bears a second meaning;
prophetic at the time of utterance, fulfilled in us
now.

It is difficult to read the words, and not see,
even if it were not intended, their wonderful
applicability to the Sacrament of the LORD's
Supper. And the Church's ancient interpretation
is not forced, which derives from them one of the
strongest proofs of her doctrine, that a partaking
of the Holy Feast is 'generally necessary to
salvation.'

In so deep a question, it is safest and wisest
to take the simplest and most natural explanation.

We go back to the first institution. The
evening before our Blessed Saviour suffered,
while He and His disciples were gathered at

their last common meal, He took bread, or rather a loaf of bread, and after giving thanks, brake it, and gave it to them, adding, 'Take, eat; this is My Body: do this in remembrance of ME.' And then took the cup of wine, and after giving thanks, bade them all drink of it, for 'This is My Blood.'

And faithful to their departed Master's ordinance, from the earliest ages, have Christians observed the solemn feast.

We call it one of the two Sacraments, or divinely appointed ceremonies, by which inward grace is pledged and conveyed to us, and by which we plight our oath of fealty to our Heavenly Captain.

What, then, is the Eucharist, or LORD's Supper?

(a.) It is a commemoration of the Death of Christ, accompanied with thanksgiving for the benefits secured by His Death. 'As often as ye eat this Bread, and drink this Cup, ye do show the LORD's Death till He come.'

(b.) The eating of that Bread and Wine is to a faithful receiver a partaking of the very Flesh and Blood of the Redeemer—'This is My Body:' 'This is My Blood.' 'The Cup of blessing which we bless, is it not the communion (i. e. partaking) of the Blood of Christ? The Bread which we break, is it not the communion of the Body of Christ?' Clearly then the Body and Blood of Christ are really present in the LORD's Supper.

But in what sense really present? Our senses tell us that even after the Prayer of Consecration the bread is still bread, the wine still wine. And when the LORD said, 'This is My Body—is My Blood,' His actual flesh was still living and unbroken; so that He could not have used the words in a literal sense. Therefore, the real Presence of Christ at the LORD's Supper is a spiritual one, invisible to the senses. Hence, none but the faithful can be partakers of Him, none but those who are enabled by the grace of GOD to feel His real Presence, and take Him into their souls; to 'feed upon Him in their hearts by faith with thanksgiving.'

Here let us stop, and seek no further. Curious and inquisitive prying will possibly do harm. There are deep things in Divine Truth which men cannot fathom. It is wiser to leave them alone. A boy, boldly venturing to cross a mountain without a guide, soon finds himself wrapped in a mist, and lost in bewilderment. We run a risk of involving ourselves in inextricable mazes if we try to supplement the teaching of Revelation. It is better to believe and worship.

Doctrinal controversies very frequently circle round the various aspects of the Sacraments, because there is so much that is deep in them, appealing, as they essentially do, to man's faith. And it is quite conceivable that different minds should entertain, without offence, different opinions in regard to points which so utterly transcend explanation. At all events, it is not charity to narrow the limits of Truth beyond the boundaries marked down in Holy Scripture; and it seems safest on the whole to take the simple words of the LORD without either adding to or diminishing from them.

Let the communicant take the sacred food as really the Body and Blood of Jesus Christ, a veritable source of strength and refreshment to the soul; and then, how it is so, why it is so, will be of little consequence—enough to enjoy true communion with Him, and substantial strength through His Cross.

Now, if the Holy Communion be indeed a partaking of Christ, its necessity cannot be gainsayed.

But you may say: Is it impossible to be saved if a man does not receive the LORD'S Supper before death?

The question is beside the mark. A really honest man does not say, 'How little may I do to get to Heaven? How near may I run to ruin without being ruined? How many excuses can be made for me?' But rather, 'Tell me what are GOD'S commands, and I will obey; tell me His ordinary methods of sanctifying man, and I will adopt them; tell me how I can best show

my love to Him, my faith in Him, and I will
do it.'

And to this objection we say : Here is a
positive injunction of our Blessed LORD, and
therefore, whatever its own intrinsic worth, you
disobey at your peril.   There are heathen, who
may be saved—men who have never heard of
Christ ; and yet, the only way of safety mentioned in the Bible is believing on the LORD
Jesus Christ.   All means of grace are in GOD'S
own keeping : He may see fit to save one who
has never received any one of the ordinary
means ; but that has nothing to do with the
other question, *viz.* If we know of the ordinary
means, and will not use them, have we any right
to expect that we shall be treated as if we had
used them ?

Were a king to offer grants of land to any
who would serve in a war for the defence of the
country, it would be a foolish question—Can we
not obtain a grant without serving in the war?
The king *might* give a grant to some who served
him in a different way, but in ordinary cases
he would not.   GOD may save a man without
the Sacraments ;   but those who reject the
Sacraments, are, to say the least, in great peril.
'Except ye eat the flesh . . . . . . ye have no life
in you.'

Again it is said : 'Many do receive the Holy
Communion without being better for it.'   Granted.

Many take medicines which do them no good, because along with them they take other things which counteract the effect: should we therefore never take medicine? Because money is often abused, is it never to be used? Mischievous publications are written; should no books on that account be issued? Prayer is mockery in the mouths of many; is it therefore wrong to pray? Neither the Holy Supper, nor any other means of grace, is a charm of infallible blessing to every receiver. Yet, though injurious to the unworthy partaker, it is a priceless boon to the devout communicant. The blessing waits for you, the enjoyment of it depends on yourself. Do not look to other people, and stop till you are sure that everybody who receives the Bread and Wine is benefited. You have to look to yourselves. To you GOD waits to be gracious.

The commonest plea of all is, 'I am not worthy, and I do not like to risk eternal condemnation by profaning so holy Food with my unclean lips.'

In passing, bear in mind that the passage in 1 Cor. xi. 29 is not to the purpose. The Corinthians were guilty of actual rioting, revelry, and breach of charity, at their love-feasts, and deserved sharp words: and the word translated damnation means temporal 'judgment,' (See margin,) such as sickness, death. (Verse 30.)

But what do you mean by 'unworthy?' Do

you mean that you are living in gross sin? full
of spite, and careless about your soul? Then, by
no means come; you *would* profane the Feast.
Yet then, bethink you whither your feet are
carrying you. Are you content to drop down
foot by foot into the great abyss, easily or
desperately? In any sense like this, if you are
unworthy, you are likewise unfit to die, and your
peril is imminent, even if you do not profane the
LORD'S Table.

But if you mean, by calling yourself ' unworthy,'
that you think that those who receive the Holy
Communion ought to be particularly strict and
conscientious, and you fear your inability to live
up to your light, or your wishes—if it is a sense
of infirmity that keeps you away—then, I am
bold to say, ' You are not unworthy; you possess
the first ingredient of fitness, a low estimate of
yourself.' It is a mistake to imagine that only
perfect saints—only very very good people—
ought to come forward; for then, who ever could
partake? and GOD would be inviting us to a
Feast which He knew that no one could enjoy
without incurring the guilt of profanity.

The truth is, the LORD'S Supper is not enough
regarded as a means of grace, a help to become
better. If it were only a sealing ordinance,
then it could only be once received, and would
then be no more needed. But it is a helping
ordinance, and is meant to meet continual

necessities—to give food; and food is a thing of every day. If you suppose that the Eucharist is received as a sign and proof that we are safe, and out of danger, perfect, and sure of final acceptance, you are under quite a wrong impression. By the Holy Supper the Power of Christ is conveyed to man's soul—strength and refreshment in temptations and sorrows. If you feel the sharpness of temptation, the fascination of sin, the difficulty of holiness—why, then, above all, you need help; and then, above all, you will find succour, if you humbly receive the Body and Blood of your Redeemer. As to fitness, anyone who is dissatisfied with sin and self, and pines for improvement—anyone who is lowly, faithful, charitable, is a fit and accepted guest at the Holy Feast.

And if I urge you on this matter, Brethren, it is because I know that you all need, and yet that many of you never dream of partaking of, this Holy Food. 'I get on very well without it: I am as good as most communicants; I say my prayers, read my Bible, am honest, and a church-goer: isn't that enough?' No: not enough, while the LORD's command is systematically neglected. You must use all instruments for preparing yourself for GOD: the carpenter needs all his tools; the gardener must do more than dig the ground and clear the weeds, he must set the seed and water it. And those who omit

Holy Communion leave their most effective weapon to rust.

Do you want command over your temper, patience in trial, courage for action? Nowhere else is it so surely to be found. For here you draw away from the world, and approach Christ; here you solemnly claim Almighty aid; here you embrace the Everlasting Arms; here you join with others, and all join with Christ. Here many have drawn deep draughts of consolation; here souls that could find no rest elsewhere, that could not pray, could not profit by Scripture, could not meditate with any sense of peace, have at last found what they panted for. Many a sick couch has been eased, and pain been made tolerable, through this Holy Feast: and often has the eye, whose brightness was being glazed over by the finger of Death, flashed out brightly once more, while feeding for the last time on earth on that sacred Bread and holy Wine. True, there is cause for trembling awe, but not for cowering dread. Keble's words are truest—

'It is my Maker, dare I stay?
My Saviour, dare I turn away?'

Some again hold this Sacrament to be appropriate only to a death-bed—that, forsooth, only when the breath is fitful, the senses unstrung, the mind clouded, is it time to 'take the Sacrament.' Ah! this is but the common folly of putting off to the latest possible time, duties which are meant for the day of health and activity; and it is the same mad presumption that counts anything good enough for the soul. Spend your life frivolously, carelessly, indulgently, and the last flicker of existence is enough to prepare the spirit, saturated with sin, and crippled with long habits of earthliness, for the purity and blessedness of a saint's death! GOD keep us from such improvidence, which only the glaring terrors of the great Day will expose!

Have you ever parted with some dear friend, perhaps never to see him again? Is there not something unusually impressive in his last request, and his last conversation with you? Do not his words linger on your memory? He has asked you to do something, immaterial in itself, but important as something to be done for his sake—would you refuse him? And if you knew he was dying, would you hesitate to promise that you would gratify his wish?

My Brethren, it was our dear LORD's dying wish that we should feed on His Body and Blood. Who dares refuse?

And this solemn week on which we are entering, when we trace His weary blood-stained path up to the Cross on Calvary—this week of sufferings, this climax of His love for us—is not a time in which, if we have gratitude, we can slight His wishes, or spurn His bounties. We must creep near to His Feet, and gaze up in His Face, and whisper, 'Speak, Lord, for Thy servants hear.' Tell us how we may adore Thee best; aid us in doing Thy Will; make us feel the power of Thy sufferings, the strength of Thy victory, that we may joyfully hold communion with Thee, and hereafter share in Thy glorious Resurrection.

SERMON VII.

CONFESSION OF SIN.

PSALM XXXII. 6. (Prayer-Book Version.)

I said, I will confess my sins unto the LORD : *and so Thou forgavest the wickedness of my sin.*

A MAN, fancying himself to be in the enjoyment of good health, may be told by a physician that there are symptoms in his case denoting some serious organic disease. I believe this to be the case with many a man in regard to his spiritual constitution : at least, looking out on the world, you will see few who have a right notion of the dangerous condition of their souls.

It is common enough to speak of sin in vague terms, to say that we are all sinners ; but men often imagine that this is a sort of excuse for them : 'We cannot help ourselves—we inherit it—it is in the blood—a misfortune certainly, but not our fault.'

5

But it is not common to see, still less to feel, the personal guilt attaching to us; to feel that our own acts are real sins, and our position therefore perilous.

What is sin? Never mind whence it came; but what *is* it? It is useless to ask how we caught the fever. How are we to conquer it? And what is sin? Not merely this or that act: but it is our acting in opposition to the Will of GOD.

We are bound by every tie—creation, preservation, redemption, adoption, daily blessings, daily tendernesses—to the LORD our GOD; to do His Will, to love His Laws, to delight in His Presence.

Therefore, not to do this, not to bend to His Will, is to act as unfilial children, as false creatures not answering to the end of their creation. And this is sin—opposing or not bending to the Will of GOD.

The devil sinned from the beginning, resisting his Liege LORD. Adam and Eve sinned because they did their own will. The Israelites sinned because they clamoured for a king, when the LORD their GOD was their King. The Jews sinned because they would only own a conquering Prince as Messiah, and GOD willed a suffering Messiah. We sin, when we would have our own wish, and crave for riches, health, peace, the world, its pomps, its pleasures, its lusts; when

GOD bids us turn our thoughts to the unseen treasures stored up in Heaven.

Hence, our first aim should be to understand the true measure of sin. Thousands of actions, deemed innocent and allowable, are yet sins, because, though not professedly done out of spite or strong rebelliousness against GOD, they are opposed to His Will. It is not only the villain, the ruffian, who is a sinner; but the man whose speech is careless, showing that he forgets the All-searching Mind; the man who is too indolent to help his neighbour, whom the LORD wishes him to succour; the man who plays with truth, or cheats his fellow; the man who omits religious duties, and sets light by ordinances which GOD Himself has taken trouble to inculcate—all such are sinners, and much more sinners than they think.

And we may acquire this sense of sin by seeing whether our wills agree with GOD's declared Will. And where this test shews a falling off, there we may detect sin, greater in proportion as we are less disposed to give it up.

It is necessary to insist on this, because sin is, whether known or not, a heavy burden to those who harbour it. You may not be aware how some underground spring is sapping the foundations of your house, yet the mischief is going on all the same, and you would be thankful to discover it.

But, supposing you know of your sin, and are
not so foolish as to blind yourself to it; how are
you to shake off its burden ?   For you would not
morbidly hug it in a tight embrace; you would
not complacently watch the tide advancing nearer
and nearer, and the rising waters cutting off your
retreat from the rock on which you stand.   How
are you to release yourself ?

There is but One who can strike off the fetters,
cancel the record of indictment, and free you from
present misery—and that One is your offended
Father.   If you are a parent yourself, and have
an erring child, you would prefer, infinitely prefer,
reclaiming to punishing him.   It may be for his
good to punish him, but mere punishment will not
reclaim him.   I think you would try to persuade
him that he is wrong, would appeal to his better
feelings, would draw them out, and work on
them; and what you would most yearn for would
be to hear a penitent voice crying, 'I have done
wrong; I am sorry; oh! forgive me!' and when
you heard that, though you might still allow the
punishment to fall upon him, because it would
help to impress his fault more vividly upon him,
yet the punishment itself would be lighter, and
your own heart not so heavy; and the child would
not turn sulky and dogged, but, feeling the justice
of his distress, would resolve on better ways.   So
would our Eternal Father take pleasure in hearing
the sighing of the contrite heart, and the desire

of such as be sorrowful for their sins; and then,
'Blessed are they that mourn, for they shall be
comforted.'

Oh! thou who dost desire forgiveness for thy
sin, confess it! out with it! conceal it not! Disguised, hidden, it works mischief; discovered, it
takes its flight, like some prowling beast that has
stolen into the house. Confess it! for the act of
confession will bring more comfort and safety
than you can imagine. 'I said, I will confess my
sins unto the LORD, and so Thou forgavest the
wickedness of my sin.'

Yet it is hard; the natural temper is proud;
we do not like to own ourselves wrong; even if
our reason is convinced, our heart kicks at the
shame of avowing our guilt. Yet, it must come
out; therefore, why not utter it with a good
grace, and be open and honest about it? It is
best to know the worst of things. A man knows
that he has a heart-disease: well, it makes him
feel the precariousness of his life, but withal, he
takes more care of himself, and thereby perhaps
prolongs his days. At all events, if he is a right-
minded person, he confesses, 'My time is in Thy
hands,' and therefore he studies to die daily, by
constant preparation for his end. Who shall say
that such an one is not a gainer?

Still it is hard to look things in the face: and
yet we must do so; we must own our sins
honestly.

1. To our own hearts—and then, down comes our pride. We thought ourselves tolerably good, and that we could pass muster as well as most; but beginning to look, we detect, here first, and then there, a blemish, an infirmity, a gross sin. It is best to be frank, and rather to make the most than the least of our faults. The iron-founder examines the huge mass of some iron girder, on which he has spent much labour; he sees one tiny crack, but passes it by, hoping, though with strong misgiving, that the real strength of the metal will not be affected; and ere long he hears that the bridge has fallen, and men have been killed by it, and that the disaster is traced to a flaw in the metal. He had better have faced the disappointment, and have had the piece re-cast, than have been responsible for the accident.

2. To others. When a man knows his own fault, he does not like others to know it: he would prefer to remain in their eyes the spotless man he once was in his own. It is a degrading thought that others should know that you have been guilty of a meanness, of intemperance, of passion, of untruthfulness; and yet by trying to conceal it from them, you may be adding deception to your former error. Not that we are bound to blaze abroad our faults; *that* might do more harm than good: but to cover them, or palliate them, so as to retain the good opinion of others, is fruitless and insincere. Bitter though it be to lose

the good opinion of friends, still even that is better than disingenuousness.

3. To GOD. It is GOD Whom we have offended: to GOD must our confession be made. I do not mean by merely joining in the words of the General Confession, with the same coldness which, alas! so many feel when repeating it at our Church Services; but with abject sorrow, and unfeigned shame that we should in any, the least, point have outraged the Majesty, the Purity, the Honour, of GOD; with body, soul, and spirit, all bowed down; with reason silent, with no excuses, no special pleading, no attempt to set off against our faults any good things which we have done; but simply engrossed in our hatred of the evil thing we have done, and unreservedly acknowledging its wickedness. Even insincere penitents, like Pharaoh and Ahab, were spared for the time because they confessed; much more may we count upon being forgiven, when the confession is one of honest sorrow of heart. For 'to this man will I look, even to him that is poor and of a contrite spirit, and that trembleth at My word.' This, but nothing else, will disarm the Wrath of GOD; this will unlock the flood-gates of His Mercy, when we so far shew ourselves His children as to confess the truth at the expense of our own pride, and by a wrench of all our natural dispositions.

Let this confession ever be ours; to lay bare before Him, 'to Whom all hearts be open,' all our spiritual failings and misdemeanours, throwing ourselves on His Mercy, and giving glory to the LORD our GOD.

And you will find, that the more readily you open up your heart, the more power you will have to scrutinize it, and the more unsavoury and ill your sins will appear. For conscience grows tender by use. The savage holds life cheap, and takes it without compunction; but made a Christian, he forswears slaughter. The Christian-born is taught to loathe murder, but he gradually learns to shun also hatred and strife, and to grieve over uncharitableness. Once open the eye of our spirit, and in time no corner of our heart will be concealed from our view.

But suppose a man cannot quiet his conscience by secret confession to Almighty GOD, what remedy remains? Then comes in the 'ministry of reconciliation.' Something human the man craves, some human voice to tell him to his face that he is forgiven, to assure him, and to dispel doubts. This is the province of what may be called, technically, Confession and Absolution. It is no superstitious form, no magic touch, no capricious human will, to bind or loose according to its own freak; but a solemn authoritative announcement to them that truly repent, that GOD pardons. Mark you, not a general announcement that GOD forgives all who repent, but a particular announcement that He forgives that special penitent. Do not be afraid of this truth, that if anyone confesses his sin to a duly authorized Clergyman, he will receive a true absolution from that human mouth. If a Christian Priest possesses any power at all, he possesses this, *viz.* of binding up the broken in heart, of preaching deliverance to the captive, of proclaiming pardon to penitents. His office is nothing if he cannot do this.

The Church of England is moderate and careful in this, as in other doctrines. She enjoins her members, if they be troubled in mind, to have recourse to some godly minister for advice and comfort, and to receive the benefit of absolution : and the Priest has no option but to declare forgiveness to him who consults him as a true heart-broken penitent : and great will be the consolation which may be so derived. But it is wisely enjoined not as a constant and necessary act of duty, but as a medicine for special cases of spiritual distress.

But 'I said I would confess, . . . and so Thou forgavest.' How rich a blessing ! Forgiven ! to feel the burden of guilt taken off, to see smiles for frowns, favour for sadness, a new course possible and inviting us.

Very different is it in the world. The culprit may be thoroughly penitent, his sentence carried out, and he released, but the stigma remains ; he has been a convict : the heartless world, wrapping itself up contemptuously in its own virtue, curls its proud lip at him : he has been a convict, trust him not. And this cold mistrust often drives him back into former wickedness.

But GOD's forgiveness is unfettered : ' Neither do I condemn thee ; go, and sin no more.'

Oh ! is not such promised peace worth all the self-humiliation, the bowing down of our pride, the consenting to be counted vile, which is implied in true Repentance.

But to the unconfessing, unconvinced, and proud-hearted, there is no peace, but that false self-complacency which ends in miserable disappointment.

Here, then, stands Christ our Saviour, calling sinners to Him. Let us try and so feel our sins that we may seek Him. Do not anyone think that He speaks not to you. He calls saints as well as sinners : ' Come to be forgiven.' If you *are* saints, you will be the first to own your deficiencies : if you cannot see them, you have not made the first step towards being saints.

Yet have faith, that, as He has promised, so if you have been penitent, He has already performed His promise, and *has* forgiven you. And then it only remains that you, because much has been forgiven, should love much, devote yourself to Him who *died* for you, and shake off, by the Holy Spirit, every evil habit, that you may rise with Him to eternal purity and holiness.

SERMON VIII.

COLLECTEDNESS OF CHRIST.
Holy Week.

St. Luke, xiii. 33.

Nevertheless, I must walk to-day, and to-morrow, and the day following.

By far the most instructive part of a man's life is the time of sorrow and trouble. Many present a grand appearance in the hey-day of prosperity— you might think them unerring and blameless— but there comes a gust of adversity, and forth-with they are but wrecks, standing out gaunt and shattered. And just as you know not the value of metal till it has passed through the fire, so you know not of what spirit a man is till he has been sharply proved. In his trial time his strength or weakness comes out; you see his temper, what he can bear, where he flinches. On a sick bed we often shew quite different colours—the good-tempered turns out fretful—the cold and phlegmatic tender and thoughtful—the religious in conversation unchristian in behaviour—the reserved, who seldom has uttered a word on serious matters, full of faith and hope, loud in GOD's praises.

During this Holy Week we meditate from day to day upon Christ in His hour of trial. In that last mournful week of His Life, the astounding depth and ineffable nobleness of His spirituality is more than ever apparent. You see Him in all the weakness of human nature, yet with all the strength of Divine power—bowed down to the very dust by the crushing burden which His Father laid upon Him; yet under all the pressure, while every weakest point is tried, and every nerve is strained almost to breaking, still bearing, still unsubdued, still upheld by the stronger strength within Him. Every action tells, every word tells. Each suffering has its own effect upon Him, each separate wound only lays open the secrets of His inner heart, and confirms our sense of His sinlessness, and inextinguishable holiness.

I would notice to-day the collectedness of our dear suffering LORD. 'I must walk to-day, and to-morrow, and the day following.' There is a calm confidence in these words, shewing how truly practical was all that He ever said. Men sometimes say that religious people are unpractical, full of ideas and fancies, but not fitted for battling with the rude world, nor for doing the ordinary business of life. There is nothing in Holy Scripture, nor in the examples of saints, to prove this. As religion is intended for common life, so the best specimens of holy persons are remarkable for the way in which they make their principles minister to their practical usefulness, and draw from their faith a living support in times when other strength invariably fails. They feel that they have a work to do, and they do it, when others would perhaps shrink from the exertion, and hunt after excuses for neglecting it.

'Jesus knew that His hour was come that He should depart out of this world unto the Father.' He foresaw the exact moment and manner of His Death, and the terrible struggles which were to precede it. He foresaw the gathering spite of His foes, the desertion of His friends, the desolate dreariness of Gethsemane, the bitterness of the Cross; and yet He was calm and collected. His Work lay before Him; He was fully conscious of its hardness; yet He did not flinch.

As He enters Jerusalem on Palm Sunday, He is not carried away by the enthusiasm of the mob. He is not intimidated by the Chief Priests from cleansing His Father's sanctuary of the pollutions of traffic.

His discourse on the destruction of the Temple is that of one who could look boldly at things, and see good working in all the judgments of GOD.

His long conversations with the Twelve breathe a reassuring calmness; a proof how well balanced His feelings were, how completely His human sensibilities were under control—and that all the sadness, pain, and certainty of grief, did not unsettle His immoveable resignation.

You mark it too in His strict observance of the Passover. Though knowing that His days were numbered, yet He omitted not to prepare to keep the Feast. Most persons would, under such circumstances, have considered it waste of time to prepare for a ceremony in which they felt certain that they could never participate. Not so the LORD. Nothing of impatience, nor of recklessness, was visible in His conduct. Among other martyrs we read of instances where the knowledge of their approaching execution has not disturbed their rest nor weakened their appetite. Bishop Ridley on the eve of his death supped cheerfully with his keeper's family, and even spoke playfully of his approaching marriage feast, to which he bade his host. Nor is it rare to see men on their death-beds calmly giving directions in matters of business, signing deeds, expressing wishes. But our Blessed LORD transcends them all in His resolute working up to the very last moment of possibility.

Look again at the scene in the High Priest's

Hall. At one end on a raised floor are gathered the Chief Priests, endeavouring to fix the charge of blasphemy upon the Holy One, while menials press round eager to spend their rough brutality upon His Sacred Person. There is enough, one would suppose, to absorb His every thought; but He can afford, even then, to watch over His own. At the farther end of the hall Peter has slunk in, half hiding himself in the uncertain light which the fire was flinging on the group of servants. He has been charged with being an accomplice of Christ, and in a moment of terrified weakness has denied it—not once, but thrice. Once already has the cock crowed; now again it crows, and then the LORD turns and looks upon Peter. Was it possible that during the mock examination and insulting cruelties, the thoughts of the Saviour should revert to His followers, and that He had been thinking all the while of His apostle's danger? Yes. 'I have prayed for thee, that thy faith fail not.' Not of Himself thinks He, but of others. Not His own misery studies He, but the danger of others. He is not anxious how to behave Himself in His arduous trial, but is watching His tempted and falling apostle; and just at the critical moment of the temptation, He turns on him that one look full of tender rebuke, which proves the turning-point of his safety.

And whence sprang this collectedness of mind? It was not apathy, nor recklessness; but arose from a conscience void of offence towards GOD and towards man.

It is sin that makes a man fret; but if you can look back, and, without any self-glorification, thank GOD for having done your duty according to your ability, and for having been enabled to love and trust Him, then your mind will not be anxious. An honest steward holds himself above worry from slander or mishap; he is conscious of right principles and faithful intentions, and is therefore willing to be judged by them.

The conscience of our Blessed Redeemer was perfectly at rest. 'In Him was no sin.' Sin was indeed imputed to Him, the world's sin laid at His door; but He had no consciousness of inherent sin. Sin's guilt, sin's punishment, was upon Him, but the sense of sinning could not be in Him. Sin was upon Him, but not in Him. 'The Philistines are upon thee, Samson,' was said with no effect while the strong man maintained his Nazarite character; but when he forgat his national and religious character, and placed himself in the power of a wicked woman, his strength was gone, and he trembled like a weak, because a guilty, man.

The LORD was calm too, because He felt that the Father was with Him.

Often have other men been sustained by a persuasion of some inward connection with the spirit world. Fatalists, like Napoleon I., counting themselves born to carry out a certain mission, have held on unwavering in their course. The Mahommedan receives his death-stroke from the Sultan's emissary without uttering a word. Amulets or charms have often given a fictitious bravery to those who have worn them.

What wonder then if He was calm Who knew that He was not alone! The mysterious desolation of the Cross, when the Eternal Father even seemed to have left Him, was not yet come : now His oneness with His Father was a felt union with immortal succours.

He was calm also, because He was putting the finishing stroke to His great Work. His toil was well-nigh over, success was almost within His grasp, and therefore His soul was at rest.

A ship has run on a rocky coast, and is momently breaking to pieces with the violence of the surf. One of the crew volunteers to carry a rope ashore, across the breakers. See him with the rope fastened to his body, buffeting with the waves—now almost sinking, now borne on the crest of a wave—now driving on towards a rock, now dexterously avoiding it—he is nearly spent, but he reaches shore : he fastens the rope, and his work is done; he falls exhausted, and dies. But he is calm throughout : he has undertaken the peril as a work of love and self-sacrifice, and he is collected and brave.

And many a one of the great benefactors of

6

mankind has said, as he died in harness, as it were, and worn out with his labours: 'Now I can die happily, for I have done my work.'

So, but in far higher sense, was it with our LORD. A few more hours, and He cries with loud voice, 'It is finished!'—'man's Redemption is complete: My Life of suffering has bought his deliverance: man is saved, My Work is done. Father, now lettest Thou Thy Son depart in peace; for Mine eyes have seen Thy Salvation.' 'He saw of the travail of His soul, and was satisfied.'

But you say, 'We can never feel that calmness.' Do not say so. We are bidden to follow in His steps, and, in our measure, we may follow.

No doubt there is much in our life to make us nervous and excited. In hours of perplexity it is very hard to look things in the face, and resolve to confront them: it is much more natural to get confused and bewildered, and then to do perhaps the very thing which you would rather not do. Men for whom you have high respect are often so thrown off their balance by sudden misfortune, as to do the wildest and most culpable things, simply from not knowing what they were doing. 'I shall go mad: my head will burst: I can't bear it.' And so the mind, by yielding to this nervous excitability, becomes more and more unstrung.

My Brethren, it is only by adopting our Blessed

LORD's principle that we can nerve ourselves for such an hour of darkness.

His mind was riveted on one thing—His Work: and so all else came like something extra and beside the question. A vessel at anchor is tossed up and down as the waves rise and fall, and veers round and round as the wind shifts, but on the whole she keeps her station. So was Christ. For His Work He lived : for His Work He suffered : for His Work He died. He was tempted ; ah ! how terribly tempted ! yet He went on with His Work. He was reviled and abused, and that shamefully; yet He went on with His Work. He was persecuted, all unjustly, causelessly, ungratefully ; yet He went on with His Work. He suffered (and who can sound the depth of His sufferings?) yet He went on with His Work. He died ; and then in His Death He finished His Work. From first to last He was working while it was *day;* and when the night came, His Work was done.

Be it so with us ! Set we our work, our truest, and most spiritual work, before us, and address ourselves to it ; and then let nothing shake our constancy, nor disturb our equanimity ; and nothing will. For as the honest fear no slanderers, so the holy fear no evil. Their trust in Christ is firm : they make His calmness their own : they hear Him say, ' It is I,' and they are not afraid. If neighbours say ill-natured things of them, and they are asked why they do not resent it, and chafe at it; they reply, 'The venom cannot penetrate my heart; the arrows fly over my head, because I am protected by a consciousness of loving GOD.'

Oh! let us fasten our memories on that calm and majestic Sufferer, as He passes to and fro among His foes, as He stands in silent meekness before His ruthless accusers, and as He drags His weary steps up the hill of sorrow to His Cross. Ye fretting and restless ones, look there! Ye desperate, or reckless, or careless ones, look there! He does His work in spite of all: take heart, and do your work likewise. Suffer perhaps you may the while, but you will not half feel your sufferings. Difficulties will vanish, if you trust to His sympathy: hard things will grow easy, rough places plain: and through all the clouds will stream some ray of the far-off light, thin and scanty to the eye of others, but full of warmth and encouragement to you—bringing a message from the Glory where the once suffering Saviour now is, a message to tell you that there is a place there for you—a glory, and a crown.

SERMON IX.

INTERCESSORY PRAYER.

JAMES, v. 16.

Pray one for another, that ye may be healed.

THE force of Prayer is undeniable. Man can wield no stronger weapon. Sennacherib's host melts away before Hezekiah's prayer. Jannes and Jambres failed to take away the frogs which their sorceries had produced, but the prayer of Moses removed the plague. At Elijah's prayer the rain came or was withheld: at Elisha's, the spirit of the dead returned to the corpse. Mountains, with their everlasting roots, must rise and depart at the prayer of faith.

We will examine into the strength of one special form of prayer, viz :—Intercession.

This is an essential element in true prayer, and is often lost sight of when people speak of a man saying *his* prayers ; as if the person praying were the only one concerned in the petition.

The Holy Scriptures lay great stress upon the duty of intercessory prayer. ' I exhort,' says St. Paul, ' that first of all . . . . intercessions . . . . be made for all men.' Samuel's words are, ' As for me, GOD forbid that I should sin against the LORD in ceasing to pray for you.' St. Paul often asked for the prayers of the Church for him, and exemplified the duty in his own person; ' We do not cease to pray for you.' Hear Moses pleading for rebellious Israel : ' LORD, why doth Thy wrath wax hot against this people ? . . . . . turn from Thy fierce wrath.' Job was commanded to pray for his three friends. When St. Peter was in prison, prayer was made without ceasing of the Church unto GOD for him.

Moreover, the principle of intercession is acknowledged in common life ; if a father makes interest to advance his son in life, or if a friend intercedes with an angry parent for a child in disgrace, or if a memorial be signed to invoke the Royal clemency for a condemned culprit.

The text implies intercession for spiritual benefits. ' Healed ' refers to recovery from sin— ' Confess your *faults* one to another, and pray one for another, that ye may be healed.' We will therefore confine our thoughts to intercession in behalf of the *spiritual* wants of others.

Is there not need in this quarter ? Who, in a world brimful of sin, has not some spiritual defect,

calling for the intercession of others? Some
may be saintly, but none is above the necessity
of a friend's prayers. St. Paul was saintly, but
again and again he begs that his converts would
pray for him. No growth in grace, no progress
in self-discipline, can supersede this necessity.
There is no Church in which there is not some
festering wound poisoning the body—some abuse,
some corrupt practice, calling for reformation.
Can you find any Order of priests or ministers
without blame in conduct or doctrine? or any set
of pious laymen above all censure? Select the
holiest person you know, and yet you cannot say,
'He is so good I need not pray for him.' But if
you could do that, still there are crowds of persons
around you, whom you love, or respect, or care
for, who have many points in their characters
which were better amended.

And beside all this, there is the vast heathen
world, dead to GOD and Truth, yet every one
among them has an immortal soul, that must be
happy or sad for ever. It is enough to make
thoughtful hearts shudder at the thought that
there are myriads of souls dropping down one by
one towards the eternal gulph, and perhaps all
because their fellow-creatures, who know better,
are not praying for them.

But here strike in two objections.

(1.) You may say, 'I am not fit: my own
infirmities disqualify me: my own sins are perhaps

greater than theirs for whom you bid me pray. Will GOD hear my prayer?'

It is quite true that it is 'the effectual fervent prayer of a *righteous* man' that 'availeth much:' true also that 'the prayer of the wicked is sin.' But nowhere is it said that the prayer of an honest, humble, not over-confident, heart will not be heard. Of course, the holier the man, the more effectual his prayer: but effectual in *some* degree will any man's prayer be, if he is in earnest, and conscious of his faults.

You are not fit to pray for others? Then you are not fit to pray for yourself. And shall you therefore not pray for yourself? Shall we wait till we are perfect before we pray? But then shall we not be beyond the need of prayer? Prayer must come from imperfect lips. And remember that in the very passage which extols the effect of the righteous man's prayer, the instance given is expressly guarded from this objection. Elias was a man subject to like passions as we are, and he prayed; ... *i.e.* though he was not perfect, but weak, yet his prayer was effectual.

Do not say that you are unfit, but strive to increase your fitness; and meanwhile, practise intercession for others as one means towards your own improvement.

(2.) Again, you may say, 'It seems like pride to pray for others. Is it not as much as saying,

I am better than that person, and therefore I may pray for him ?'

No doubt the habit, so sadly common, of denouncing the sins of our neighbours, is simply the result of self-righteousness : the raking up all the slips and transgressions of others does make us often very proud : it is the Pharisee over again, 'GOD, I thank Thee. . . . .' But intercession is a very different thing. Probably there is nothing which contributes so much to enlarge our sympathies, and open our hearts, and stifle our prejudices, as to kneel before GOD and solemnly to pray for another. The highest recorded instance of Love and Humility is that of the dying Son of GOD, when He said, 'Father, forgive them.' And true intercession is not a prayer that others may be like us—GOD forbid ! —but that they may be made like Him, our great Example.

And now what are the benefits of Intercessory Prayer ?

(1.) To others. There is a promise to this, as to every other kind of prayer—'Ask, and ye shall have ;' therefore, if we seek according to the Will of GOD, we shall find. Now what is more in accordance with the Will of GOD than the saving of the sinner, the Sanctification of the careless, the strengthening of the feeble in spirit ? For GOD would save all, hallow all hearts, and strengthen all the weak : and therefore if we pray for such things, we may expect an answer in His good time.   He only knows, how many a poor silly wanderer has been brought back by the secret prayer of some interceding friend ; how many an obstinate offender has been checked in the height of his sin by the operation of the unknown prayers of someone whose advice he has often scorned.   Perhaps in the mid career of his guilty course, just on the verge of committing some black crime, he has felt a sharp twinge of conscience, and has bethought him of those early days, when his soul was still untainted with deliberate sin, and he had listened to the gentle guiding of a mother's voice, whom he has long deserted and well-nigh forgotten.   May it not be that she who has so often mourned over his fall, but never lost her love, has been perpetually pleading at the throne of GOD for her erring child, and now, at last, that indomitable prayer has touched the ear of the Holy One, and He has sent His Spirit to rouse the dull and death-like soul, and give it one more chance of repentance.   The great Father, St. Augustine, declares that under GOD it was owing to his sainted mother Monica's unwearied intercessions, that he was turned from sin and error to the light of truth.

Indeed, we cannot prize too highly such loving pleadings : the more so, that they can avail when other means have failed, or are impossible.   The

wicked may scorn advice, entreaty, rebuke; but
they cannot break away from the reach of the
Christian's prayer for them, nor resist the influence which that prayer directs against them.
Intercession bridges over all space, rank, circumstances, place, even time itself: for it is a spiritual
power, which leaps right on to a spiritual end,
and draws down with it a spiritual help. Man
may resist the storm, the earthquake, the wind,
the fire; but the heart cannot shut out the still
small voice.

And what but the Holy Spirit, with His still
small voice, can arrest or awaken the sinner? If
then we have invoked His co-operation, we have
struck a victorious blow for our friend, under
which alone the Evil Spirit will quail. Therefore,
though prayer is.a resource when all other means
are unavailing, yet call it not a last resource, for
it is a master-key which no locks nor wards can
baffle.

(2.) To ourselves :—To begin with, it is an act
of prayer, solemnizing our thoughts, kindling our
faith, giving a more vivid sense of GOD's presence.
Then, in calling to mind the faults of others, we
naturally recollect our own. Hardened hypocrites
must we indeed be, if we kneel down before the
LORD at such a time, only to gloat over our
neighbour's iniquities, and quite forgetful of our
own. Surely it will be more natural, while we
entreat the LORD to remove this or that fault in

our friend, to join with our prayer one for the removal of our own sins : and the more hearty our intercession, the sharper and more distinct will come out the outline of our own faults, and we shall perchance find ourselves to be guilty in the very same point where our neighbour seemed so to fail.

More important still will be the impulse given to our charity. The very act of intercession is an act of love; and the more we cultivate our love, the more fully it will unfold itself. I am sure there is no way so effectual for stifling animosities, or encouraging affection towards those with whom the Providence of God has cast our lot, as the habit of remembering them before God. Suppose you had, rightly or wrongly, quarreled with a relative, and you felt angry words rising to your lips, and you turned away and lifted up a silent prayer not only for yourself for patience, but for the other that he might be reconciled ; malice could not find shelter in your breast, you could not enter the man's presence again without recollecting that you had prayed for him, and that thought would make you patient and self-controlled. And therefore it is a wholesome rule, at the first birth of angry feelings to pray for him who has displeased us ; and that prayer will prove like David's harp to Saul's unquiet spirit.

Consider then what would be the effect, if the

whole Christian Church exercised persistently the power of intercession. The national sins, the delinquencies of those in power, the struggles of unprincipled schemers, the fierce controversies on religion, the innumerable petty vexations and heart-burnings of domestic life, would all but die out, when so many earnest voices were raised to the GOD of Love, pleading for the reformation and sanctification of others.

Surely the Christian's part is not to cry down or cynically abuse men in office, but to pray for their guidance in justice and equity : not for the laity and clergy to criticize one another ; but to pray for one another, that there may be faithful pastors and docile sheep : not for parents to ill-treat or neglect their children, nor for children to scorn or ridicule their parents ; but the one to pray for the other : not for the pious to turn their backs on the disorderly, but to pray for them. In this mutual intercession is one sign of true Church-membership, and one main source of strength and patience.

Will not the thought that others are at this very moment mentioning our names before GOD inspirit us in withstanding temptation ? And should not we bestow the boon which we receive ? We know not how much may be depending on our individual petition. Some wayward child of GOD may be at this moment wavering between good and evil, his eternal destiny quivering in the balance, and possibly (who can tell?) one single prayer of ours for him may draw down the turning weight of grace, and a soul may be saved. Is not the bare chance of such a blessed event enough to encourage us to pray incessantly for others, if the LORD should so ordain to save one soul for our unworthy prayer? And on the other hand, shall we suffer any one soul to be lost, simply because there is no one to care for it, to pray for it?

There is One Who is ever praying for us: He never tires: we are ever in His Heart. 'Father, I will that they also whom Thou hast given Me be with Me where I am.' It is for us to prove our likeness to Him by praying to '*Our* Father,' not only for ourselves, but for our brethren, that our dear LORD's prayer may be fulfilled in us all.

SERMON X.

PROMISES.

Psalm cxlvi. 5. *(Prayer Book Version.)*

Who keepeth His Promise for ever.

Looking at the shifts to which careless people are driven, the crooked schemes, the foolish unprincipled devices, to which they have recourse, and the failures to which they are subject, one is amazed that they should overlook the only reliable source of help; and the Psalmist's words come forcibly to mind: 'Blessed is he that hath the God of Jacob for his help, and whose hope is in the Lord his God, Who made heaven and earth, the sea, and all that therein is; Who keepeth His promise for ever.' Often had David proved the hollowness of human friendships, the feebleness of human aid, the deceitfulness of human promises; and well might he say, 'O put not your trust in princes, nor in any child of man; for there is no help in them.'

This Psalm extols the faithfulness of the LORD, as the Protector of the weak and oppressed, the Restorer of liberty, the Recoverer of lost senses, the One Who cares for His righteous children. GOD is not a man, that He should lie. . . . Hath He said, and shall He not do it? 'So shall My Word be; . . . it shall not return unto Me void.' Since He is Truth, Light, Love, and Justice, how can He not keep His Promise? His Word is true and sure, for good or evil, for mercy or judgment.

1. For judgment. He is no capricious tyrant; nothing short of obstinate rebellion provokes a judgment from Him; and therefore, when He does pronounce judgment, and the time is fully come, irresistibly swoops the sword of vengeance. The Flood, the overthrow of Sodom, the annihilation of Babylon, the fall of Jerusalem, the dispersion of the Jews, are all instances in proof; and seeming exceptions are only seeming. Though Nineveh was spared, GOD's Truth stood firm. It was Nineveh, case-hardened and impenitent, that was threatened; it was Nineveh, conscience-stricken and penitent, that was spared, because, for the time, the condition was changed, on which all Divine threats are issued, viz., impenitence. GOD threatens the wicked; and

while he continues wicked, the punishment is inevitable; but when he repents it is waived.

Similarly the unbeliever's scoff, 'Where is the promise of His coming?' may be answered. GOD delays to destroy the world. So He did in Noah's time, but the Flood came. He delays coming to judge now, but He will come. He 'is not slack concerning His promise, but is long-suffering,' to give all, even the wicked, a greater chance for repentance. All the converging lines of GOD's decrees are gradually drawing to the centre; all the marvellous springs and intricate wheels which move the Almighty's designs, are little by little working out the great result; it is coming—it must come. What are a few thousand years to the Eternal, but the momentary pulses of time hastening with rapid throb to its consummation?

2. For mercy His Word is sure also. 'His mercy endureth for ever.' 'I have sworn once by My Holiness that I will not fail David.' 'GOD is faithful, Who will not suffer you to be tempted above that ye are able.' 'He is faithful and just to forgive us our sins.' 'I have been young, and now am old; and yet saw I never the righteous forsaken.' Have seed-time and harvest failed? Have summer and winter stood still in their round? Have we had cause to doubt the return of our labours? The failure of his crops one year does not dishearten the

7

farmer; temporary ill-success does not make the merchant less diligent. And if we hear of some cases of starvation and death by famine, our attention is only all the more fastened on the rule, that men do not die of famine, that bread and water do not fail. Ourselves are living monuments of GOD's constancy to His Promise.

Or, looking deeper; has His Promise failed, that those who seek the inward peace shall find it? Is there one, honestly longing for a quiet conscience, who has not felt some comfort flow through the Holy Spirit? Is there one who has not (it may indeed be with delays) found the dark clouds of doubt clear away as he struggled to penetrate them, and gaze on the brightness behind? His grace is ever sufficient; and over troublous seas, that run mountains high, against adverse winds and currents, still has our vessel sped on, and still does our compass shew that our course is true; when we are with GOD, He is with us.

Pass we from the faithfulness of GOD, to the faithfulness of man. GOD's children should be faithful to their word. Fidelity, wherever seen, is admired. The Roman general, Regulus, having been taken prisoner, was paroled, with permission to go home, on condition that he should advise his countrymen to accept the terms of the Carthaginians, and failing the attempt, return to his captivity. His patriotism forbade him

giving such advice, but his honour bade him
return to the enemy, though he clearly saw
that there was no alternative but death, perhaps
a cruel one; and this his ungenerous foes inflicted
on him. We boast that the world respects (or
did respect) an Englishman's word; we are right
to count it an honour. Against the duplicity
of Eastern nations, and lying statecraft of some
unprincipled politicians, we are right to exclaim.
How much more should a Christian Englishman
abide by his word, scorn to say one thing and
mean another, to make promises never to be
performed! 'He keepeth His promise for ever.'
Be it ours humbly to follow in His footsteps,
and to speak the truth from our hearts.

And if in all points, so specially in promises.
A promise is an undertaking to do something,
declaring our solemn intention to follow a particular line of conduct. When we have made
a promise, we should keep to it. And why is it
binding? (1.) Because of *truth*; it is inconsistent
with truth to 'alter the thing which has gone
out of our lips.' That 'sea of glass, clear as
crystal,' which St. John saw spread before the
throne of GOD, is a fit symbol of the purity of
truth; and we shall never be meet to look on
that glorious sight, if our tongues can frame
falsehood, and carelessly make declarations
without any intention of fulfilling them. (2.)
Because of *others*; if we have passed our word

to another, our promise implicates him; we have put ourselves in his power, and on our promise, he, perchance, has built up his own plans, which would be disarranged if we fail in our promise. Our word has been trusted; hopes have been raised upon it. If we fail to carry out our promise, mistrust springs up as well as disappointment; we cannot expect to be listened to again. The men of Jabesh-Gilead never lost a strong feeling of gratitude to Saul, because he had kept his promise of succour, and had raised the siege of their town by the time appointed; and when the corpses of Saul and Jonathan had been shamefully nailed to the Philistine walls after the defeat on Gilboa, they performed the daring feat of carrying off the remains and decently interring them. Consider in a military campaign, how the success of the movements planned by the commander-in-chief depends on each divisional commander fulfilling his engagement; let only one sleep over his duty, and the whole army may suffer defeat. Or if a messenger is sent ashore *from some disabled ship, with a promise to procure help, and once landed, pays no more heed to the matter, disaster is the consequence. Or a man lends a sum of money on the faith of a promise from the borrower to return it by a certain date; the loan is not repaid, and the lender is perhaps unable to meet his own creditors. Such promises affect many more besides the promiser himself.

Sometimes the promise is only *implied*, but still it is binding. Between master and servant there is an implied engagement, that each will discharge his duty to the other; between parent and child; between members of the same club or society; and in many other relationships into which we enter, fully aware of the obligations connected therewith. We cannot shirk the obligation, nor abjure the responsibility, because the promise was not given in so many words. Where you go among others in a certain character, knowing that they so regard you, and act on the faith of your being what you seem, then if you are not what you seem, you act deceitfully, and do harm to others. A pointsman on a railway, who is not punctual at his post, breaks an implied promise, just as much as if he had said that he would mind the points for the particular train which has run off the line. A Christian, by his general profession of serving GOD, undertakes virtually many duties, the neglect of which is to break his implied promise.

A promise on oath is much more binding. A vow made on oath may not be uttered hastily. An oath is a solemn assertion, invoking the Name of GOD, to Whom an appeal is thereby made to confirm the truth of what is said; it being supposed that what a man utters, feeling himself to be in the presence of GOD, and fearing His Majesty, is more likely to be truth. But if this solemn adjuration be made, it must only be in a serious and good cause—in a court of law—on taking some weighty or sacred office; but never lightly, never for evil, never to set a seal of blasphemy on some wicked thought. But when the pledge is so given, it becomes all the more binding, because made in the presence of the Searcher of hearts.

But is the sacred promise kept? Is an oath between man and man reverenced? Is not the poet's dispirited language too true?

'Constancy dwells in realms above.'
Coleridge.

Let us consider.

But first. Is an oath always to be kept? No; there are vows, made in moments of rashness, 'more honoured in the breach than the observance.' It was an evil moment for Herod, when he vowed to grant Herodias' daughter anything that she might ask. It was a still worse moment for him, when he kept his vow, and gave her the head of the holy Baptist; for that was not only to commit a murder and sin himself, but to inflict a fatal injury on another. An ill day was it for the wild judge, Jephthah, when he solemnly vowed to offer to GOD the first living thing that should meet him after his victory; but murder, or its equivalent, was worse than a broken vow. These men read us a lesson in their reverence for a vow, although they are not to be copied in their rashness and want of moral courage.

(*a.*) General promises. When once we have pledged our word, see that we rigidly adhere to it; the voice of promise, so often inconsiderately uttered in worldly transactions, is echoed above; and He Who is Truth grieves, when the promise is only voice, has no root in the heart, no seriousness, no deliberate resolution attached to it. Can a man's word be depended upon, as it should be? Is there not a sort of slipshod way of saying 'I will,' which makes trade, and the ordinary intercourse of life, very untrustworthy? 'I will meet you at such a time and place;' 'I will send you what you order by such a day;' 'You may rely on my executing your wish immediately;' and oftentimes such expressions are merely to parry attention, and give an impression of activity and diligence, which is never thought of any more. Depend upon it, no dealings with others in the most trivial affairs can ever prosper when there is so great a disregard for our promise. Honesty belongs not only to fair charges, but to engagements and undertakings also; a contract binds, whether there be a deed in writing to attest it or not.

(*b.*) Implied promises. The sponsor's pledge

is an instance. In his own person he says nothing; he does not *say*, 'I will see to this child, and bring it up in the fear of GOD, as far as rests with me;' but his being present to answer in the child's name is as much as to say it; and if he does not endeavour to lead his Godchild to holiness, by example and precept, he neglects his duty.

(*c*.) Solemn vows. Take the marriage vow as an example. There are flagrant misconceptions abroad in regard to the obligation of the marriage vow—why, I do not know, if those who enter into wedlock would only meditate beforehand on the step which they are about to take. The man and woman plight their troth to each other, for better for worse; there is no exception made, no qualification; the man does not say, 'So long as my wife obeys me, I will cherish her;' the woman does not say, 'So long as my husband is kind to me, I will love him;' no; it is a simple solemn compact, made before GOD and the Church, that, come joy, come sorrow, they will love one another to their lives' end. Ah! surely the recollection of such a vow ought to, and would, if allowed to remain, check either party in a temptation to unfaithfulness, or in a bursting out of anger. Surely, if the married pair felt that they had made an eternal vow to be one for ever, we should not hear of divorce, of separation, of bitter quarrels, of constant

bickerings and irritation. The marriage bond
would be venerated, the home love would grow
warm; the longer the union, the warmer the
love—the older in years, the closer in heart;
then, too, the solemnity of the vow might from
time to time stir up spiritual thoughts, and
remind husband and wife that they were walking
in the sight of God, before Whom they had
once joined hands and pledged themselves to an
irrefragable union. Would that, before they are
married, men and women would ponder well 'the
holy estate of matrimony,' and consider that the
vow is irrevocable; and so, entering upon this
new relationship in the fear of God, win His
blessing, and win His grace, to follow them in
their journey through life.

'He keepeth His promise for ever.' Think of
this, Christians! And as sons of God, think
of your Christian vows! You were baptized,
and then was made an implied promise that you
should love God for ever. Later in life you
were confirmed; thenceforward God's vows were
upon you; you deliberately chose good and
rejected evil. Oh! keep your promise, keep it
for ever; keep it in spite of sin and self, and
the world, and Satan; keep it, by the exercise
of every grace, by the use of every spiritual
help; keep it, until Christ Himself sets His
seal upon it, by taking you to His Everlasting
Rest.

And whenever you make resolves in the strength of GOD, as the temptations of the enemy thicken, make them with the full purpose of carrying them out with faith and earnestness. 'Promise unto the LORD your GOD, and keep it, all ye that are round about Him; bring presents unto Him that ought to be feared.'

It is refreshing to look from this deceitful world of false friendships, of underhandedness, of ever-broken promises and violated vows, to the unswerving truthfulness of GOD, Who never faileth them that trust Him. There, at least, we are safe, and may anchor securely.

Did you ever taste the bitterness of broken faith? the heartlessness and thoughtlessness of human pledges? Did you ever know what it was to be betrayed by your friend? then you, at all events, will prize our Blessed Redeemer's promise: 'I am with you alway, even unto the end of the world.'

Be ye true to your promise to Him. As for Him, 'He keepeth His promise for ever.'

SERMON XI.

PEACEMAKERS.

St. Matthew, v. 9.

Blessed are the peacemakers : for they shall be called the children of God.

Everyone has felt the beauty and pleasantness of a bright calm day in autumn, when everything around is mellow and soft, and the soul is stilled by the stillness of nature. True, in a boisterous gale there may be something invigorating and exciting, when the winds roar, the trees sway to and fro, and the waves dash high—it is a grand sight, stirring the soul ; but the other has perhaps a more powerful influence. There is that in it, for which the inmost spirit of man pants more than for aught else : and there is that in it, which is a true reflection of the mind which animates heavenly beings. Angels at Christ's Birth sang 'Peace on earth.' Messiah Himself is 'the Prince of Peace.' We address GOD in our Liturgy as 'the Author of Peace.' And the very word 'Peace' sounds heavenly : just as it sounds unnatural and incongruous that 'there was war in Heaven.'

And if the thing itself is so good, those who promote it and help to spread its influence must be engaged on a blessed work : even as Blessed above all others is He Who came to bring peace on earth.

I take 'Peacemakers' to mean those who 'seek peace and ensue it,' and whose object is to introduce peace wherever they are, and upon whatever they are working, and with whomsoever they hold intercourse.

1. Peace should be in our own soul ; therefore, blessed are those who make peace for our own soul. Our natural heart is at war with GOD : the New Birth alone does away with the enmity. Naturally, man regards GOD as a tyrant; His service bondage. To be holy, is with him to be miserable : he cannot bear the restraint of resisting evil.

> 'Licence they mean when they cry liberty.'
> *Milton.*

He must be taught to discover that GOD is a Father, and that only his own corruption blinds him, and distorts his sense of what is right and delightful. It is only the Spirit of Christ who

can effect this : and Blessed indeed is that Spirit
when He thus becomes the Peacemaker, recon-
ciling man to His GOD, through the Only-
begotten, the true Mediator : and blessed is he,
too, who shall, by help of that Divine Spirit, win
so great a change for his soul. If we become in
this sense peacemakers to ourselves, it must prove
a blessed thing indeed : all the horror, all the
aversion, all the restlessness, all the thankless
dissatisfied thoughts, which belong to the wicked,
are swept away, and in their place there breathes
peace. The stillness of a trustful heart, of a
patient hope, of a confidence in GOD's Love, in
spite of all we have done or are doing to displease
Him, will be a sensation worthy to be called
blessed. If it be not ours now, my Brethren, let
us never rest till we have sought for it, and
gained it.

2. Peace towards men should reign in our
minds. It is a part of true Christianity to 'be at
peace one with another.' 'Where envying and
strife is, there is confusion and every evil work.'
And where we are true children of GOD, we must
copy Him 'who maketh men to be of one mind
in an house.' I need not to dwell on the miseries
of enmity; it were a rare fortune indeed not to
know the effects of jealousy, distrust, bitterness,
and quarrels. To be instrumental, therefore, in
dispersing such evils, to try to feel kindly towards
everyone, and to persuade others to feel kindly

towards each other, is to behave as a true bene-factor to the human race, and is a blessed thing, for which we cannot be too thankful. There is no denying the difficulty of becoming such a peacemaker; it is implied in the Apostle's words, 'If it be *possible*, as much as lieth in you, live peaceably with all men.' We may feel charitably ourselves towards others, who may refuse to reciprocate the feeling. Indeed, history records how the noblest of earth's benefactors have in-curred odium, roused by their very goodness, which the eyes of envy could not tolerate. So, too, it is a thankless task to endeavour to reconcile those who are at variance; for we have then to step between a man and his prejudices, or his anger, to both of which he obstinately clings, while chafing at any interference. Yet it is not always a hopeless undertaking. Firmness, bold-ness, with at the same time lovingness, are powerful influences, especially with those who are being carried away by passions, for such persons are often very impressible by the coolness and collectedness which they do not enjoy themselves. And, provided we do not burst in at an unseason-able juncture, we may greatly further the restora-tion of peace.

3. Peace should inspire the Church. In GOD'S own Family above all others should prevail peace and amity. Oh! what an outrage is it upon our fair fame as the Church of Christ, linked in holy

union with the Prince of Peace, when there are such divisions among us!

Of course, in the diversity of human faculties, and of circumstances, much allowance must be made for varieties in our modes of Christian life and thought. It may be quite justifiable that we should have favourite doctrines, or ceremonies, according to natural tastes, or a sense of different weaknesses or necessities. One can conceive that the Church in a warmer or a colder climate should think more or less about external rites, or that different branches of the Church Catholic should have different liturgies; and again, that one individual Christian should be inclined to press more on the doctrine of the necessity of works, or the necessity of faith; that one should wish to warn others against intemperance, another against covetousness, just because it was that sin which had been most mischievous to himself. But all these and similar points should be recognized, and not allowed to interrupt the peace of the Church. Men are fond of coining telling watchwords for themselves, without holding to the Bond which may unite all parties. They seem to suppose that the existence of parties in the Church helps to deepen its life and energy. And certainly very few seem to be able to work heartily for the general object of Truth and Love universal. The more's the pity!

Now surely the existence of parties in the

Church, though it may represent zeal, does not always tend to edify. Many a lukewarm Christian has gained fervour by espousing a party cry; but the fire which he has inhaled into his spirit inflames dormant passion, and makes him full of jealousy and self-importance, without at all kindling a truer Christian spirit. Zeal of this temper is not to be desired; it promotes nothing but bigotry, and narrows the mind of him who possesses it. There seems a great lack of catholic spirit, and of that openness of mind which can comprehend differences of thought, taste, and circumstance, which lead others into a different groove from that in which we ourselves are running. When we find that one, who has been brought up to worship GOD according to a plain ritual, is not only unable to enter into a more elaborate ceremonial in a Church service, but is positively disturbed and angered by what, after all, does not affect vital points, surely there is something wrong. Or, again, when a person accustomed to choral services cannot endure to take part in any service colder or less musical; here, again, is something wrong. But when these private dislikes lead to open opposition, lead (as they have often led) to rivalries and mutual denunciations, lead to bitter animosity; who can deny that there must be something wrong, very wrong? The spirit of our gentle loving LORD dwelt most on men's good qualities and hopeful characteristics. The young ruler was seriously in fault, yet 'Jesus looking upon him loved him,' trying by kind advice to improve those habits in him which *were* good. He thought it no straining of truth to say of His relentless persecutors, 'Father, forgive them, for they know not what they do.' To the woman taken in adultery there was a pity in His words, a kindness in His sternness—'Go, and sin no more'—for He brake not the bruised reed. They that are Christ's, therefore, should 'believe all things, hope all things,' of others. Wherever we see zeal and earnestness, though it be not according to knowledge, we should bear them record, and give them credit for it, and not denounce their ignorance, and ignore their fervour. In practice, what I mean is this. We have in the English Church a number of different schools— parties, if you will—never mind their names; the less they are mentioned, the better. Now, are we to confine our intercourse rigidly to what we consider the most correct and orthodox? Are we bound to wash our hands of everything which those who do not agree with us do for GOD's honour? There is no blessedness promised to the unbending and exclusive, but there is to the peacemakers. Granted, there may be important differences, involving serious questions of doctrine; still, unless these doctrines are vitally opposed to the spirit of the Gospel, there are surely sufficient points of agreement for us to clasp hands, and

8

work harmoniously together. And blessed shall
we be if we promote this better feeling. Certain
I am that the more distinctly and strenuously we
put before our minds the one object at which we
all ought to aim, the more our eyes will be shut
to the minor differences between others and ourselves. Do not think that I mean to say that
differences are trivial, and that it matters not
what we believe or practise; but there is such a
thing as holding the Truth, as we receive it
according to our light, in love.

So, too, between Churches. If reunion can be
brought about in Christendom, GOD speed those
who are pleading for it! There may be funda-
mental errors in a Church; and with such a
Church, until those errors are renounced, union is
impossible. But it is as unkind as it is unfair to
blame those who are endeavouring to smoothe the
way to reconciliation, or at least to throw out
feelers as to whether there be any disposition on
the other side to make some concessions. 'Blessed
are the peacemakers.'

O Brethren, let us yearn for peace in Christ's
Family, and long for the time when we shall be
all one, and the one Fold shall embrace all the
sheep. And may we not then expect that the
desires of many hearts shall beget a spirit of con-
cession and forbearance, which, without sacrificing
truth, or countenancing error, may pave the way
for more union, based upon a warmer love for

Christ our LORD—when Protestants and Roman-
ists shall find some common ground of faith—
when all the various parties in our own Church,
and all the manifold sects of Christians in the
world, shall be able to discuss their differences in
a spirit of true loving-kindness, and with a sincere
desire only to approve themselves children of
GOD ?

'O pray for the peace of Jerusalem !' Pray
for the spirit of concord, at home, and in the
Church Catholic. Pray for that secret peace
which passeth all understanding. Pray that
Christ may so dwell in your hearts by faith, that
your zeal may be tempered with charity, that self
may be swallowed up in large-heartedness, and
that, while drawing your own peace from the
LORD Himself, you may live in peace with every
fellow-creature.

SERMON XII.

CHILDREN.

St. Matthew, vi. 9.

Our Father . . . .

A consciousness of having offended produces fear : and fear paralyses reason and enfeebles hope. And this is one reason why barbarous nations have recourse to propitiatory sacrifices— their fear drives away any sober reflection, and they have not nerve enough to examine into the true disposition of Almighty God—all His terribleness stands out in ghastly relief, overdrawn and exaggerated, while His tenderness is quite concealed from view. It is one province of true religion to dispel misconceptions of God's character, and to turn such a light upon His attitude towards man, as shall reveal Him to us as a Father. Let us consider this relationship, and some lessons which may be deduced from it.

(1.) GOD is our Father, as the Source from which our life, and the nourishment of our life, is derived. Anyone considering what is required for the sustenance of our body, the unremitting care, the momently protection, the controlling of accidents and perils, must recognize in our daily existence an unmistakeable proof of the kindness of that great Being, 'in Whom we live and move and have our being.'

(2.) GOD is our Father, in His Love for our souls. He Who could not bear to see us perish in our sins, but in His wondrous wisdom conceived and executed a scheme for our deliverance—has well earned the title of our Father. That He should sacrifice His own beloved Son—that He should send forth the comfort of the Holy Ghost, flowing with gifts and graces of power, tender in His warnings, faithful in His checkings of our sins—that He should be the author of our spiritual life, our spiritual sustenance, our spiritual joy, is a still stronger evidence that He is a loving Father : and most fitly does our LORD put into our mouths this title as the dearest and most effectual, as He bids us, when we pray, to say, ' Our Father.'

From the Fatherhood of GOD we may draw two lessons :—

(1.) Our duty to Him, our Father ; and
(2.) The general duty of children to their parents.

(1.) If GOD be a Father to us—that is, watches over us, giving growth to our bodies, recruiting our spent strength, cheering our languor, rousing our depression, enabling us to feel the freshness of life, renewed to us every morning;—if He supplies sustenance for the wear and tear of spiritual life; not only telling us how to be saved in His Son, but drawing us by supernatural means into union with His Son, feeding us with the Bread of spiritual meat—then, what do we owe Him for it?

Love—deepest warmest love: gratitude—fullest heartiest gratitude: expressed in those fervent petitions of the LORD's Prayer, 'Hallowed be Thy Name, Thy Kingdom come, Thy Will be done in earth, as it is in Heaven.' That should be our first wish of all—before we wish for benefits to ourselves, before we ask for daily bread, or even pardon of sin—that GOD's Fatherly Name may be honoured as It deserves.

And more yet. To our Father's service we should consecrate our best powers; to His Will yield implicit submission; for His Wisdom is infinite, therefore it is folly to disobey Him; His Love is unbounded, therefore it is heartlessness to disobey Him. At His feet we should delight to lay all that we have, desiring only to do what He wills, to be what He wills—to be dutiful and loving children, to walk according to His disposition, and to suffer His character to leaven all the feelings of our hearts; that is, to be sons of GOD, like Him, after His Image.

(2.) From the Fatherhood of GOD we may consider the *general duty of children to their parents.* Some perhaps would derive our duty to GOD from what they would call the natural instinctive duty of the child to its earthly parents. I am inclined to think that we ought to argue the other way. True, parental authority is the origin of all government, and earthly authority; but parental authority itself has its origin in GOD's Fatherhood. He was Father to man before ever a child was born on earth; and human fathers and mothers only take their relationship and authority from Him. We should not say then, because children should obey their parents, therefore the children of GOD should obey their Heavenly Father; but because GOD is our Heavenly Father, and claims filial obedience, therefore should we shew filial obedience to our earthly parents. It is not, Love GOD as we love man; but Love man as we love GOD. To GOD all our first obligations tend, in GOD is the centre and spring of all true earthly relationships; and if we could only religiously observe our duty to Him, all lower duties would naturally follow, and be necessarily included.

Our filial obedience to GOD then reminds us of our filial obedience to our parents. Every right-minded child of GOD will acknowledge the obligation of filial obedience to his parents; 'He who loveth GOD, love his brother also.' As the Tabernacle was to be constructed on the pattern shewed to Moses in the mount; so after the same fashion (of course in lower degree) in which we regard our heavenly, should we regard our earthly parent.

But too clearly sin makes this an irksome duty. The Prophet Malachi speaks of an alienation of children from their parents, which the preaching of the second Elijah was to overcome : and still we see that Christianity has not subdued the world, since this filial piety is so rare a thing among us.

So rare a thing! Am I not justified in using the expression? Is there not a strong spirit of independence, which poisons the thoughts of the child towards its parent? Look round among your acquaintances. Can you trace in each home, among children—young or grown up—a glowing tone of filial love? Once let the child feel himself above dependence on his parent, and oftentimes affection seems gone; all former benefits wiped out of memory; reverence, kindliness, love, honour, obedience—all those qualities which the child should feel—which the Child Who was brought up at Nazareth displayed in *His* character—either unknown altogether, or greatly diminished, or kept in check by other and selfish motives, so as to be practically dead. No man can defend this : it is inhuman, not to say un-

Christian, and betokens an ignorance of that sonship, which we enjoy as children of GOD.

Doubtless we may account for it, but excuse it we cannot.

In one rank of life, young persons are so soon able to earn wages sufficient to support themselves, that feeling no longer dependent on their parents, they set them aside; and when the parents come to need assistance, it is too often refused. It is one thing for a swarm of bees to cast off from the parent and separate for ever; it is another for rational creatures to forget ancient obligations, and to act as those whom St. Paul describes as ' without natural affection.'

In another rank, school or college life, calling forth the skill and talents of the young, rouses a spirit of self-reliance, and a distaste for old habits, and as they are pleased to call them, the old-fashioned notions of their elders; and they come home with, in some cases, a sort of contempt for a father's wisdom, and a restless impatience of a mother's endearments. But if it is so, it is because the mind is ill regulated : it is no necessary result of mingling with the young of their own age. Men may reap the full advantages of college life, the emulation in study or sports, the contact of mind with mind, the rubbing off the rough edges of prejudice or temper, without in the least being compelled to throw off the gentle domestic yoke, which should be pleasant to bear. Self-will may lead us, as it did Rehoboam, to adopt very foolish counsels, and certainly is not a quality to boast of.

Nor can any change in situation or home cancel the debt which the child owes the parent. If he pleads that he has a wife and children, how does that excuse him? The heart is naturally expansive; the more objects to love, the more love we can shew. The strings of a harp are capable of being struck in endless combinations of harmonies; a skilful hand can draw forth fresh notes, where a rude player can strike but one. But in any case, there is no warrant for saying that a man must disengage himself from all former friendships, and sweep his heart clear from all natural ties of affection, before he can admit another set of affections. The more we love, the more we can love. Marriage need bring no antagonism into the heart; and the early affection for our parents need never, nor ought ever, to be extinguished, though fresh relationships spring up. GOD is the author of real and holy Love, and whatever love has His sanction is consistent with every other love which He sanctions.

Let sons and daughters then cherish reverence for the person of their father and mother. Surely there should be a something in the most familiar of all faces to secure our loving honour. We may well have learnt after so many years of closest intercourse to trace lines of beauty in countenances, which to other eyes appear plain and homely; and as age creeps on, and we shift places, and they who once supported now lean, the very helplessness which is coming over them increases their claim to our reverent assistance; and the child that can have the brazen effrontery to discard and despise the aged friends, and more than friends, who bare him in their arms when he was an unconscious infant, deserves, and must receive from all right-thinking Christians, pointed reprobation. Did Shem and Japheth lose reverence for Noah, when overcome with wine? Did Abraham shake himself loose from Terah? Did David scorn Jesse, because he himself was a warrior, and a sweet Psalmist of GOD? Did Jesus Himself despise His mother, the Blessed Virgin? Far from it: and so, that we are physically stronger, mentally wiser, spiritually holier, is rather a reason why we can well afford, without lowering our dignity, to bear with their infirmities, and turning our eyes as much as possible away from their faults, fling a decent veil over what in our hearts we think worthy of condemnation.

And it is just here that filial respect becomes so difficult. The hoary head, if found in the way of righteousness, we can easily regard as a crown of glory in anyone, and more easily still in a parent: but when the parent is evil, shews injustice, ill-temper, favouritism, it is very hard to maintain

an equal feeling of reverence and affection. Yet
no distinction is drawn in GOD's Law between a
duty that is pleasant and one that is not. We
are not at liberty to practise agreeable virtues,
and forego irksome ones. Rather, it is the unpleasant duties, which we should make a point
of discharging. And if the father or mother be
froward, harsh, censorious, tyrannical, the child
must still bow submission, (unless the call of some
higher duty intervene) and the grown-up son or
daughter must meekly bear with the unkindly
spirit, return a gentle answer to the sharp and
peevish, and be content for Christ's sake to tend
the helpless : and this, though, all the time,
misunderstood or browbeaten ; honouring the
sacred relationship, even though personal respect
is so apparently impossible. Pleasant is it to see
the little child nestling lovingly in the mother's
bosom, the boy running happily by his father's
side, the infirm mother hanging on the son's arm,
the exhausted father succoured by a devoted
daughter. But pleasanter still to see some gentle
daughter drooping with the perpetual drag of
incessantly ministering to a fretful, dissatisfied,
contemptuous parent, who exacts perfect devotedness with thankless indifference and discontent :
or a son, coming down from his pedestal of strength
or learning, to bend to the infirmities of a father,
bigoted, prejudiced, and intolerant ; stifling all his
personal feeling, waiving all his personal comfort,

in the one wish to soothe that father's last moments of life, and to dispel every breath of seeming opposition.

Sons and daughters, hear me! When a parent is in question it becomes us ever to give way, saving only when a sacrifice of principle is involved. Deal tenderly with those, but for whose care, under GOD, you would not have arrived at this stage in your earthly journey. It may be granted, looking at them as men and women, that they may be foolish, intemperate, prejudiced, and all the rest: it may be granted that you are personally infinitely their superiors: but still, all said and done, they are your parents, and for the love of your Heavenly Father, you are bound to love them and please them to the utmost: and to do this, you must shew, in your manner, tenderness, thoughtfulness, meekness; 'Honour thy father and mother.'

One other point, and I have done. The text speaks of 'Our Father, which art in Heaven;' then, where our Father is, there is our Home; and therefore Heaven is our true Home. And in Heaven can be found no wrangling, no contemptuousness for inferiors in intellect, no retorts, no exulting over inferiors in strength or ability: that Home is peaceful, a haven of rest, where jarring opinions, bitternesses, and misunderstandings, are no more. Our Father there is so transcendently superior to all His reedemed sons,

that they will not be able not to honour Him.
His Will shall be, I say not law to them, but
their will.   His Honour shall be, I say not dear
to them, but *their* honour.   They will be true
sons, whose hearts are one with their Father : and
no ' Commandment with promise ' will be needed,
because no inclination to resist will remain, where
the spirit of Satan, the Arch Rebel, can never
more find entrance.

But oh ! if we cannot draw the outline here,
how shall we ever fill in the full portrait there ?
If we honour not our parents on earth, how can
we honour our GOD ?

By His Fatherly care, therefore, let us provoke
one another to dutiful love towards our earthly
father and mother : delighting to shew, by our
affectionate and reverent treatment of them, that
we ever bear in our memory our Father in Heaven,
Whose Love feeds and blesses us every instant,
and alone can satisfy us eternally.

SERMON XIII.

PARENTS.

EPHESIANS, VI. 1, 4.

Children, obey your parents in the LORD, *for this is right.*

Ye fathers, provoke not your children to wrath, but bring them up in the nurture and admonition of the LORD.

I HAVE spoken of the duty of children towards their parents, grounding a lower duty on a higher—the duty towards the earthly on the duty towards the heavenly Parent. I will now, with GOD'S help, treat the reciprocal duty of the parent in a similar way, and from GOD'S treatment of us His children deduce the fitting behaviour of human parents towards their children. What He is to us, should we, in our measure, be to our children.

Christian duty is not one-sided—(and this seems one proof of the Divine origin of Christianity)—it

is not partial, but takes in all aspects, all relationships.   This increases the difficulty of expounding
it, because the several bearings and tendencies of
the case are to be all considered : a narrow-minded
man only looks at one side of truth, and so sees
no difficulty in following a plain downright course.
A king from his royal point of view may not
understand any hindrance in the way of absolute
submission on the part of his subjects; but the
catholic spirit of Christianity recognizes mutual
duties, and the true course of morality lies in
taking the balance between all, in the king
considering the people, and the people the
king.

Thus, the rule—' Children, obey your parents in
all things,'—must have certain limitations, to be
settled by the corresponding duty of parents
towards their children : for the absolute and
despotic control of children cannot be admitted.
A general has a right to perfect obedience in his
soldiers only in military matters.   A bishop has a
right to canonical obedience in his clergy, but is
not an infallible autocrat, whose mere will is to be
law.   Similarly, obedience to parents must be
tempered by other moral and holy obligations.

And in saying, as I did, that the child's duty
to its parents is to correspond with its duty to
GOD, I did not mean that the same implicit
obedience is due to them which is due to GOD,
but that parents stand in a sort of natural position

as deputies of our Heavenly Father, to whom, because deputies, we owe allegiance, but of course only where they demand what is in accordance with the Will of Him Whose deputies they are. At the same time, our compliance with their wishes must not depend upon our notions as to what is reasonable; but where the demand may be unreasonable, so long as not immoral, not sinful, we owe them reverence. This is, I think, borne out by the manner in which St. Peter speaks to servants: he does not say, 'If your master is unjust and exacting, or does not act as a master should, you then need not obey his orders;' but he says, 'Servants, be subject to your masters with all fear: not only to the good and gentle, but also to the *froward.*' Similarly, filial duty is not to be measured by the justice, reasonableness, or high principle, of the parent, but by the higher standard of conscience and loyalty to our Heavenly Father.

But I pass to the parent's duty.

Almighty GOD's fatherly treatment of His children is the model on which the earthly parent must frame his treatment of *his* children.

(1.) Discipline is needed. This is an essential part of real love.

There needs not to tell of GOD's Love, beaming out in all His acts towards us, undying, undeviating in its tenderness. But since His children are wayward, from the root of sin lying

9

in the heart, oftentimes His Love can only be shewn by chastisements. 'Whom the Lord loveth He chasteneth.' It were no love to let the child run its head against evil. If you saw your child in danger from fire or water, would you not snatch it to you—nay, if needful, bind it tightly to prevent it doing itself an injury? and that, not because it would be pleasure to see the little limbs writhing and fretted with the cords, but because even that sight, though painful, is less painful than the other. This is the reason why men sometimes suffer in this life. Sickness, sorrow, disappointment, strike to the very quick of the soul, to awaken it, or check it in some course which is hurrying it on to ruin. Thus the profaners of the Holy Supper at Corinth were judged in the flesh, that their souls might be saved in the Day of the LORD.

Here then lies our path, if we are parents. Eli the Priest is strongly censured because he did not restrain his sons when they made themselves vile. True, he had remonstrated with them, but he might have gone further: as a father, and the High Priest, he ought to have deposed them from the office which they profaned, and so have stopped the gross scandal of their wickedness. And Eli is condemned by the judgment pronounced upon his house.

No parent should shrink from this duty. When his child falls into evil habits, or bad company, it is not enough to persuade him to better things; he must forbid such conduct. If he refuses to go to school, compulsion must be used; if he resorts to evil places of amusement, he must be sternly prevented. It is mistaken kindness to suffer the child to have his own way; for the seeds of that selfishness and self-will are then laid, which bear fruit of sorrow both to parent and child. Those who spoil their children have much to answer for, and bitterly will they rue their folly: the spoilt child becomes the tyrant of the house, loses all respect for father and mother, and goes out into the world expecting to rule others as it has done its parents, and is always peevish and disagreeable to those around. Hence it is that when age is blanching the head of the indulgent parent, all filial affection has been so deadened by the cruel process of indulgence, that sons and daughters behave like strangers, or worse than strangers, in their inhumanity. Nor should it be forgotten, as matter of fact, that there is more real affection felt towards a firm and strict than towards an indulgent parent. Hophni and Phinehas, when they came to crouch for a piece of silver or a morsel of bread, would, I doubt not, have been the last likely to share their pitiful dole with aged Eli: and among ourselves, the first to neglect an infirm father or mother will be the child whose will has never been curbed or thwarted.

And let not parents fear to take their stand. They have a right, nay, lie under an obligation, as holding a sacred office under GOD, to lay down laws for their children, to restrain them, by force if necessary, from running into evil, and to discipline them by strictness in the paths of right and godliness.

And if this is done early, it is done easily. Make it your determination never to be conquered, but to require exact submission from your child from the very first, and, provided your own rule of life is good, you will be almost sure to succeed. It is said, and not without great show of reason, that what the child is at three years of age, it will continue to be in after life. At all events, it is certain that its after life is greatly influenced for good or for evil by the training of its infancy. Do not think it unkind to discipline your child; do it, kindly of course, and your love will grow, and the child's too. Never give an order without well weighing it first, and always in dependence upon GOD's guidance; but when once given, do not allow it to be slighted.

I am speaking chiefly of young children. It is difficult to define at what time manhood or womanhood exempts the child from the duty of filial obedience. From reverence surely never, and from obedience only when other duties clash with it.

We must add, however, that the rules which we

impose we must observe : otherwise, if we lay heavy burdens on them, which we will not touch with one of our fingers, our strictness is thrown away ; for none are so quick to see inconsistency or injustice as children, therefore make a point of being an example of fidelity to your own laws : and so

(2.) 'Provoke not your children to wrath.' All angry feelings must be suppressed, if we would rule our families in strictness. Sometimes when a boy has done wrong, the father strikes him ; the blow convinces the child that his father is out of temper, and then respect is gone, and *his* temper is roused. Judgment should be given impartially and coolly; and therefore we should never chastise children at the very moment of the fault, lest passion get the better of us, and we punish more to vent our own passion than for the child's good. When we shew an imperturbable calmness, children have no excuse for resentment : but the least sign of ill feeling stirs up ill feeling : 'iron sharpeneth iron.' There should rather be a sadness in our punishing, to assure the child by our manner how we grieve to inflict pain, and that nothing short of a stern sense of duty influences us.

The danger of displaying temper is a strong argument against corporal punishment, generally. I do not deny that there may be cases requiring it, but at any rate these are the exceptions, and it

is not always easy to use the rod or the strap
without shewing temper. Moral punishments
seem to me to be the safest and most un-
objectionable, and if judiciously applied, the most
effective.

And the punishment should not be prolonged,
nor repeated : let it be adequate, and proportioned
to the offence; but having once dealt with the
offence, we should restore the offender to his
former position, and not exclude him from our
affection. One knows of cases where the punishment is repeated over and over again : this is very
unwise, and discouraging to the child. Every
criminal should have ample opportunity of re-
covering himself : let him once feel that the
door is closed against reformation, and he grows
reckless. The convict at large, who feels the eye
of the police ever upon his movements, loses self-
respect, and knowing that no one trusts him, he
ceases to trust himself; his struggles for better
feelings and amendment of life cease, and he
becomes desperate, and at last reprobate.

But there is another point of vital moment.
Our Heavenly Father, through the Person of His
Incarnate Son, brings home His Love to each of
His creatures. With each of us He carries on a
loving sympathy, the only true link which binds
us in union with Him. Christ came on earth to
learn the fulness of sympathy, and fully did He
display it. And thus the mind of GOD is charged

with compassion and tenderness for man, willing to make every allowance for infirmities, willing to cancel the past, to brighten the future; anxious to draw out the nobler affections and aspirations, to win the love of man for Him who first loved us.

On this ground must parents take their stand. The true relationship between them and their offspring can never be fixed in its proper position, unless there vibrates from one to the other the true chord of sympathetic love, of mutual interest. There must be in this holy and natural relation the same principle which is needed in the Church, a oneness of heart and mind between the members of Christ's Body; if one suffer, so must the other, if one rejoice, so must the other. The warm glow of Ruth's words should inspire and refresh the hearts of both: 'Whither thou goest, I will go: and where thou lodgest, I will lodge; thy people shall be my people, and thy GOD my GOD. Where thou diest, will I die, and there will I be buried: the LORD do so to me, and more also, if aught but death part thee and me.'

It is the want of sympathy—thorough, open sympathy—which is the cause of mismanagement on the part of parents. Many, though truly conscientious, fail for lack of shewing sympathy: their rules are made not on the principle of kindly parental interest, but of duty, viewed in its coldest aspect. Surely it is quite intelligible how such a system should fail.

It is from the neglect of sympathy, that misunderstandings so often arise between different ranks. But for this neglect, 'strikes' and 'lockouts' would have no existence. Rebellions, usurpations, wrongs, all spring from want of sympathy. But in the relationship we are considering, sympathy is more than in any other indispensable. The father, once a boy himself, should know what boyish feelings are, should be able to bend himself down in some degree to his child's level, should not be too exacting, but should regulate the expression of his wishes so as not unnecessarily to jar with the boy's desires. In the choice of a profession for him, supreme indifference to his taste or predilection soon dispirits the lad, and has not seldom incited him to leave his home, and foolishly throw himself on the world, by enlisting in the army, or embarking in a wild speculation on his own account. Why should there not be a thorough understanding between father and son? The son's welfare must be the wish of a true father, and he would sanction any project that was not perfectly foolish and wrong. It is for the elder to make advances: but there ought to be no difficulty in this, if from the first the father claims to be the depositary of the boy's feelings and wishes. If men talk as they do of the evil of 'confession,' here is a way in which a man may be a natural confessor to his son. Let him encourage the boy to bring his

little troubles to him, never to be ashamed to tell
him of his faults, to be perfectly open with him,
and to feel certain that his father has a deep
interest in everything in which *he* is interested.
Were this habit begun early, probably many a
misdemeanour into which a youth falls might be
set right, if indeed the remembrance of the father
would not rather keep the boy out of mischief
altogether. And as he grew on in years, the
father would be always the first to be consulted
in perplexities; a wish for a profession, a love
attachment even, would be confided to one, in
whose heart the son always felt that he had a
place.

So too with the mother: girls are allowed to
enter the world in all ranks, without bearing in
their hands, as it were, the leading-strings of a
mother's sympathy. Once gone from home, the
young servant too often has no kind bosom friend,
whose constant and tender guidance would often
keep her straight. Independent and uncared for,
how can you wonder if she loses one by one,
simply because they were not taught her by a
sympathetic teacher, the lessons of religiousness,
honesty, and modesty, of which she heard in her
youth? And in a higher walk of life, young girls
mingle in society, the sport of triflers, who for an
hour's amusement will sap the foundations of their
self-respect, until in an unguarded moment they
are brought into alliance with men of no principle,

and their after life is a wreck of what once were bright hopes. Is not a mother's sympathy needed here? Let her shew herself interested in her child's welfare, hedge her round with all possible safeguards, give her healthy and useful employment, teach her to confide to the maternal heart all her little troubles and sorrows, her difficulties, her feelings towards those around. Let there be perfect openness between them; and then when the least breath of anxiety arises, there is a bosom where the young maiden heart may nestle, pour out its deep thoughts, and draw gentle counsel and relief.

Beyond question—were this high principle of sympathy felt, as a transcript and shadow of the divine sympathy of our Heavenly Father, to be the ruling principle of fathers and mothers—the practical difficulties which now arise, the heart-burnings and misunderstandings found in some families, would all be smoothed away; and if it was necessary that the parent should thwart the wishes of the child, the child would feel that it must be necessary, having perfect confidence in the love and wisdom of its parent. There would be no domineering exercise of parental authority, every check would be lovingly administered, and the child's wishes would be consulted, where feasible, and the parents would gain reverence in the eyes of the child.

Here then I would sum up the whole matter.

The relation between parent and child is mutual, the obligations mutual, and the love should be mutual. Control lovingly exercised—reverence willingly paid : each ready to give way a little, and so together falling into the course of the golden mean, of complete and harmonious sympathy. Both relationships are creations of GOD; both must be viewed in connection with the Fatherhood of GOD towards His sons; both must be carried on, on a holy and high principle, 'in the LORD.' If fathers and mothers in their behaviour remember how GOD treats His children; if sons and daughters in their behaviour remember how the children of GOD should demean themselves towards Him; then will a deep tone of piety animate the one and the other, and the relation between them on earth will be so maintained as to prepare them for their heavenly relationship. And those who love GOD as their first and truest object of love, will have the justest, deepest, truest, warmest love for their earthly relatives.

SERMON XIV.

AUTHORITY.

St. Luke, ii. 51.

And He went down with them, and came to Nazareth, and was subject unto them.

The Epiphany of our Lord unfolds His two-fold Nature. By the miracle at the marriage-feast at Cana, Jesus manifested forth His *glory;* the incident mentioned in the text was a manifestation of His *lowliness.*

When twelve years old—the time at which Jewish lads usually came forward to take their place as willing and conscious members of the Church—'the Child Jesus' accompanied Mary and Joseph to Jerusalem at the Passover season.

The Festival over, His Mother and her husband joined the long train of worshippers returning northwards to Galilee, supposing that the Child was in company with some of their acquaintance; but He tarried purposely in the Holy City.

Having discovered their mistake, they rapidly retraced their steps, and after three days search, found Him (where perhaps they should have first sought Him,) in the Temple, sitting in the midst of the doctors, both hearing them and asking them questions.

It was customary for the Rabbins to seat themselves in one or other of the chambers attached to the court of the Temple, and gather a class of young learners for catechetical instruction; and Jesus had joined one of these classes, and was listening to the expositions of these learned teachers, and putting questions of inquiry to them. It was not, be sure, to parade His own wisdom, to exercise His intellectual authority, or to puzzle them with hard questions, but to learn. 'Jesus increased in wisdom.' And thus He manifested His lowliness.

The manifestation of His glory confirms our faith; that of His lowliness braces our courage. When we feel our pride swelling within us, and its tenacity of life as we try to mortify it, and when we almost despair of mastering it, the sight of Christ's lowliness proves how pride may be mastered. He in Whom is perfect wisdom, before Whose intellect and mental powers the Gamaliels and Nicodemuses of those days were but children, yet condescended to learn of them.

Again; afterwards He returned with His parents to Nazareth, and was subject unto them, obeying their instruction, reverencing their authority, submissive to their wills.

Not for nothing did He so bend Himself, but partly to feel the effort of submitting His Will to an inferior, partly to shew how reverence should be paid to all, who by GOD's Providence, whether in natural or social positions, whether as natural guardians, as authorized teachers, or as elders, had the rule over Him.

How does our LORD's conduct speak to us? His principle, as a Man, was to accept His social position, to recognize the hand of His Heavenly Father as the mover, planner, disposer of all things. He acquiesced in His rank and relationships, in His required subordination to others in reality infinitely His inferiors, on the ground that it was His Heavenly Father's Will.

Self-will would have prompted Him to follow His own bent and inclination, to assert His own inherent rights, and to claim submission to His higher intellect and deeper spiritual insight. But had He done this, His great work of humiliation would have been incomplete; He would have shewn power without suffering, would have been a conqueror without being a victim; and so no atonement could have been made, no sacrifice offered, no blood spilt, no redemption secured for condemned, sin-laden, perishing, human nature.

Our Blessed Saviour's example then, teaches:

1. That children should subject themselves to their parents. This, however, is not the point which I wish to urge now. It is generally admitted. But those who admit this are loth to admit the kindred duty of lawful authority. They will unhesitatingly assent to the law which enforces filial obedience, but hold that maturity of age constitutes an exemption from such submission; at all events, that the duty must not be extended to any other than parental authority.

2. Consider, then, how our LORD's example affects our relations to all authority.

Ours is an age when men suffer themselves to set at naught the wish of those placed over them. It matters not what shape authority takes; imperial, civil, ecclesiastical, social, domestic; the very fact that it is authority, a defined right to command, is enough to stir up resistance.

It is very easy to concoct excuses and reasons why exceptions should be made in this case or that case; still the principle remains, that there is such a thing as lawful authority—a divine institution, ordained for the welfare of the world.

Reasonable persons cannot dispute the necessity

of constituted authority; the evils of anarchy are too plain. Nor would anyone dispute it, so long as authority did not clash with his own will. Many, who have been rebels themselves, are very eager to enforce the law against those whom they wish to coerce—a proof of the innate recognition of the propriety of law and authority.

And if Holy Scripture has any weight, there can be no doubt that we are bound to obey those set over us. 'The powers that be are ordained of GOD; .... whosoever resisteth the power, resisteth the ordinance of GOD;' here is *civil* authority. 'Obey them that have the rule over you;' here is *ecclesiastical* authority. 'Servants, be subject to your masters;' here is *domestic* authority. Nay, the principle is carried far deeper. 'All of you be subject one to another;' here is a kind of abstract authority residing in our Christianity.

But in our self-will, we shut our eyes to these plain laws, refusing to endorse the various ranks and gradations of life. Our manhood, forsooth, is to imply an immunity from law, an independent right to act as we think fit. We are far readier to ask, 'Why is this the law?' than 'What is the law?' And so right law is measured by our own will.

In England especially, our freedom as Christians and Englishmen is often much distorted, as if it countenanced insubordination to any law

of which we did not approve. But said the Apostle,
'Use not liberty as a cloke of maliciousness.'

I am not pleading for blind servility: a man
may hold his opinion, and take all fair measures
to procure an alteration in an unpalatable law;
but while it is law, he is bound in conscience to
obey it.

And not only as regards laws actually laid
down, but as regards persons vested with dis-
cretionary authority, we are too inclined to be
rebellious against the exercise of their authority.
Doubtless, many such persons are not all they
should be—have infirmities, partialities, short-
comings—still they are in authority. And to
their authority reverence is due. Holy Scripture
draws no distinction between able and feeble
magistrates, between just and unjust judges,
between godly and wicked kings, between good
and froward masters; but simply demands strict
reverence for their position, their office.

But we must confess that there is a great lack
of respect for living authority, station, and rank.
Possibly it may be said that this disrespect has
arisen from the unworthiness of the men in station,
and that worthy men will always command respect.
I do not think it quite true: it is more probable
that men are glad to lay hold of so good an
excuse for resisting what they dislike. The
true cause is self-will. We will not submit.
Who are they, to lord it over us?

10

Is not this the true cause of that sort of self-opinionated manner of many young people of both sexes now-a-days? They will not tolerate the opinions of their elders, much less brook their commands. The men of riper age are supposed to be behind the times, not sharp enough to keep pace with the rapid march of intellect! Things might be all very well, and passable in days gone by; but no one dreams of such things now; we are more enlightened!

Our Blessed Saviour might, with far greater show of justice, have said so, but He did not. His Mother's and Joseph's will was law, where not at variance with His Heavenly Father's Will.

Again, reverence for appointed teachers should be deeper than it is. Christ listened to those who sat in Moses' seat, receiving their instructions as those of servants of GOD, enabled by His grace to give sound instruction. Is this the usual feeling which pervades the minds of the laity of the Church? Are the words and admonitions of the clergy received as the message of GOD? By some, certainly: but the more usual treatment of sermons and ministerial advice is measured by the personal worth of the minister, not by his office, except in a very trifling degree. True, if a pastor can add personal influence to the dignity of his office—if, as well as being a deacon, he is a Stephen—then, his power for good is unbounded. But this does not affect the reverence

due to his sacred function : and it is above proof,
that if the lay members of the Church would
bring themselves to acknowledge the dignity of
the ministry, they would hear in the stammering
words and unlearned utterances of inferior priests,
a sound coming from above, a Voice louder and
more impressive than man's voice, a Voice strong
to touch their consciences, and bring them upon
their knees. Oh! Brethren, I ask not reverence
for myself, but for the office, which Christ Himself has instituted, and to which He has promised
the talisman of power, and the spirit of penetrating
persuasion.

Nor do I exempt my own order from the
duty of submission to authority. I see among
fellow priests too much of independence, too
little deference to the godly admonitions of the
Bishops set over us. It seems indefensible,
although often called conscientious scrupulous-
ness, and fidelity to truth; and is probably the
fruit of the same self-will which I mentioned.
Might not our Redeemer, Who said, 'The Son
of Man is Lord also of the Sabbath,' Who came
to give a fresh interpretation to the old laws and
canons of the Jewish Church, and to stir up a
new principle of spiritual life—might not He
have stood on His rights and superior knowledge,
and set all regulations and orders at defiance on
the plea of conscience? Yet He was baptized
by John, at twelve years went to His Con-

firmation, attended the Synagogues and the Temple. So, methinks, those who are appointed priests in Christ's Church should yield true obedience to those set over them. I marvel at any clergyman not complying with his Bishop's advice, even if his own judgment does not agree with it. A man who preaches up reverence to the clergy and to authority, ought himself to lead the way in yielding to his superior. A Bishop is as fallible as another man; but those who profess to acknowledge his office, should yield him due submission. I say this with special reference to a Bishop's interference to obtain more uniformity and canonical strictness in the administration of the public services.

Trying it may be, in these various ways, to man's pride to subject his own opinion and will to that of another; but it must be done. Yet there is scarcely any nobler act, than for a man of stupendous learning or talent to allow another to take precedence of him simply because he holds an office delegated, to him. It is a noble thing to recognize law as above brute force or intellectual power, and that when it thwarts his own will. True manliness is shewn in submissiveness. It is unmanly not to have moral courage to acknowledge lawful authority, and to humble our own wills.

For here lies the cross which we have to bear —the subjugation of our self-will. It may take years to subdue it, but it must be tried. Our will must not only succumb to the Will of GOD, but condescend to the will of man; which is in one sense more difficult, because we can conceive GOD's Will to be perfect and wise—man's we may know to be foolish and imperfect. But for peace sake, and for conscience sake, to shew our sense that it is GOD's Will which orders human rank and station, and therefore that it is GOD's Will that those in authority should be obeyed, we must bow our will to that of those who are placed over us.

Could we all do so, we might see an end of many long struggles, many discussions and unseemly brawls. We should at all events learn obedience, and so best fit ourselves for power and dignity, when that should come to us. And as we should contribute to the peace of society and nations, so would our inward peace be more enduring.

Oh! teach us, holy, humble Saviour, to submit ourselves, as Thou didst, to those whom our Heavenly Father places over us! Teach us to be subject with Thee, that we may reign with Thee!

SERMON XV.

DISCIPLINE OF FAITH.

St. Matthew, xv. 25.

' Lord, help me!'

God is not always indifferent to the wants of those whom He seems to pass by—He often *seems* so, but never *is*. You notice one in great poverty, struck with sickness, his life a cheerless one, full of sources of anxiety. He seems both in body and mind shut out from the great Eye of Love, uncared for, unthought of. Is it so in truth?

You see the earth tightly bound with frost, as if all its powers of fertility were gone; but the effect of the frost is beneficial, not to say indispensable, to the productiveness of the earth.

So with man. Poverty makes him anxious, murmuring. Sickness tries his temper. 'What cares God for me?' he may say: nay, 'God has a spite against me.' And yet, side by side with the burden he is bearing, stands the gentle spirit of discipline, shewing the emptiness, the transiency, the mischievousness, of all things of earth; shewing the weakness of human nature, and its complete dependence upon Some One beyond itself.

And thus, though body and mind suffer cruelly, the seeds are sown of a feeling of self-diffidence, and spirituality, which elevates the character, and prepares it for better things.

So was it of old. Jehovah seemed to give all His love and thought to Israel: the Jews received the chief blessings, outward and spiritual: the Gentiles were almost ignored: no Divine laws, no inspired prophecies, no revelation by Urim and Thummin, were vouchsafed to them. Yet GOD had not forgotten them.

Every here and there along the line of Jewish history we come across an instance of some good quality being noticed among the Gentiles: Jethro, Ruth, the Queen of Sheba, foreshadow a truth afterwards to be more fully declared, that GOD would send 'a light to lighten the Gentiles.'

In later times of Jewish history we find the same. Our LORD's mission was in the first instance to the chosen people. His charge to His disciples was, 'Go not into the way of the Gentiles: and in no instance, it is believed, did He pass the boundary of the Jewish provinces. But as the swift rolling river hurling itself down some deep fall swerves not from its course, and yet flings its spray upon the edges of its banks; so did our Blessed LORD, while keeping to the track laid down for Him, and personally not going into Gentile provinces, still here and there throw off some of His boundless blessings on Gentiles who came as near as they could to Him. 'For in every nation he that feareth Him and worketh righteousness is accepted with Him.'

The text recalls a case in point. Our LORD, with His disciples, had approached the borders of Tyre and Sidon. The report of His miracles had preceded Him, and among others was heard by a Syro-Phenician woman whose daughter was possessed with a devil. She hurried in search of Him, though doubtless aware of the exclusive spirit of the Jews.

Jesus, to avoid the public gaze, had entered into a house: but she sought Him out, and at once falling at His feet, entreated pity for her daughter.

His treatment of her exactly bears out what I said of GOD's seeming indifference sometimes to human suffering. 'He answered her never a word.'

His disciples seem more kindly: 'Send her away, for she crieth after us:' in other words, 'Heal her daughter, and let her go.' But there is a touch of selfishness in their charity: they wished to be rid of the poor creature's teazing importunity. How like ourselves! It is easier

to give than to say no : and so we often seem
charitable, when we are only stopping an annoyance. And thus many undeserving imposters
carry off the alms, which belong rather to the
deserving but more retiring poor. Let judgment
rather guide our charity than selfishness.

Our LORD's reply to the disciples is not more
promising to the poor mother. 'I am not sent,
but unto the lost sheep of the house of Israel ;'
not to the Canaanites.

But she is not so easily discouraged. She
grows bolder. 'Then came she and worshipped
Him, saying, LORD, help me !'

'Surely now He is opening His mouth, and will
grant my prayer.'

But no : His words are chilling. 'It is not
meet to take the children's bread, and to cast it
to dogs.'

Yet if those words are chilling, not so His
manner, else had her lips closed for ever. Faith
has an eagle eye, piercing dark and undistinguish-
able shadows, and discerning the object of its
search where others see nothing. She knows
Christ better than to retreat now. She will try
once again.

Truth, LORD : I admit the inference : I *am* a
dog, an outcast, and despised : I merit not the
favour I ask, I frankly own it : but I know the
Love of GOD is infinite, and as the dogs have a
right to the crumbs beneath their masters' tables,

so have I and my daughter, in virtue of being
GOD's creatures, a title to the remnants of the
heavenly feast, to the overflowings of the rich cup
of blessings; and Thou wilt not deny me so little
as that. I am sinful, yet art Thou merciful and
gracious: and I know that Thou wilt hear me, yet.

His seeming sternness is gone: she has won
the day. 'O woman, great is thy faith: be it
unto thee even as thou wilt.'

Now, why all this reluctance on Christ's part?
Merely to play with her feelings? God forbid!
Never did our dear LORD say one word, which
could imply want of consideration for anyone's
feelings. And never should we allow ourselves,
either for the sake of shewing our power, or
testing our influence, or amusing ourselves at the
workings of the sensibilities of others, to forget
to study their pleasure and peace of mind. A
man of thoughtless speech often wounds most
deeply. And if we would only remember how
we ourselves have smarted under unintended
thoughtlessness, we should be careful to give no
occasion to others to writhe under inconsiderate
words of ours.

His silence first, and His seeming roughness
afterwards, was meant and proved to be a true
kindness. He was trying, confirming, and com-
pleting, her trust in Him. Without faith we
cannot please GOD, nor secure His blessings.
This poor mother was in woeful need, for soul

and body, for herself and her daughter: the deeper her faith, the more her blessings would be; and therefore our LORD put her faith to the proof.

Was that unkind? Are parents unkind, who teach their children many things against the grain, because they know what pleasure the knowledge of those things will bring afterwards? They put them through the drudgery of learning the rudiments of music or painting, for they are sure that the after gain far outweighs the trouble of learning. Is it cruel in the surgeon to bind up the broken limb so tightly, or to put the patient to the pain of probing the wound, so that nothing may be left, which may inflame the sore or retard recovery?

And was it unkind in Jesus to make as though He heard not, when He knew that this, far from driving the suppliant away, would only draw her on, and enlarge her faith, and so make the gift when given tenfold more precious? Could He give her a greater blessing than faith, which would prove a very spring of perpetual blessings? To have used it once, and felt its power, would be to her an earnest of continual success, whenever she had a prayer to offer. She would be able to say, 'Once by my importunity I obtained my suit: I will ever be importunate till an answer comes.'

How often would such thoughts comfort us,

if we could feel them in our needs? The
Tempter whispers: 'God cares not for you! See!
people often pray, and never an answer comes;
none will come to you; you had better waste no
more time in praying: He is stern: you speak to
the heedless air.' No, no: Brethren, it is not so!
Is GOD so unwise, so unkind, that you cannot
trust Him a little, nor wait a moment? He only
wants to make you long for Him more; He does
not mean not to answer. 'Shall not GOD avenge
His own elect, which cry day and night to Him,
though He bear long with them?' Push on your
cause, more vigorously, more earnestly, and you
shall prosper.

But mark the mother's earnestness. Is it not
because we are so cold in prayer, that we receive
no answer? Is it likely that GOD should bend
His Ear to a casual unthinking petition? Why
are we to pray at all? Not to inform, not to
persuade Him, but to evidence our allegiance to
Him, and to shew ourselves sensible that we
depend on Him. Our needs are all exposed to
His view, yes, before they come to us. We speak
not to the dull hard rock, that cannot hear, cannot move, but to a spirit of love and goodness.
He is ready: it is for us to shew ourselves ready.
This is why we pray. Hence, if there be no
fervour, prayer is useless: if no pertinacity, no
real craving, it is no prayer. If you would be
heard, be earnest.

How can we look for answers to our rapid, unfelt, formal prayers? Much and often speaking is not prayer: asking again and again is not prayer: the body without the spirit is not more unprofitable than prayer without heart. The wrestling Jacob should rather be our model, the importunate widow in the parable, and this woman of Canaan. Five minutes in the morning, five sleepy minutes at night, are not samples of successful prayer, which GOD would love to answer. We should (1) feel what we want, (2) meditate on Christ—His power, His willingness, (3) gaze on Him, watch His manner of dealing, wait for His time. Were we to study GOD's ways more, (not with a prying curiosity, but with humble docility,)—see how He acts, whether He is wont to grant requests at once, what temper He looks for, what is His usual course in answering or not—we should learn experience, and experience would beget hope.

But after all, the whole matter turns upon this. We do not cry, 'LORD, help me!' from our hearts, because we do not feel that we require help. We are content with the outer crust of ceremonial, bending the knee, clasping the hands, closing the eyes; and so we may never have proved what the reality of a prayer is, from never having felt our necessity. Ask the hearts of most men of business whether they have ever cried, 'LORD, help me,' with a conviction that, unless GOD did help them,

they were lost. The regular routine of ordinary
and honest trading has stifled the searching of
their mind, and made them fancy that respect-
ability was godliness. No wonder they have
never prayed fervidly; they know not why they
should pray. They are satisfied with sobriety,
and the absence of glaring vices such as society
would condemn. They have not measured their
spiritual height by the measure of the stature of
the fulness of Christ, to find themselves like
grasshoppers by the sons of Anak, dwarfed and
deficient in their love of divine things. On the
other hand, they do not understand the greatness
and majesty of GOD, the purity of Heaven, and
the complete change which must come over their
minds, before they can be fit to enter there. But
oh! if they could but discover it, and see how
deeply the disease of sin is eating into the very
life of their souls, they would soon cry out with
heartfelt concern, ' LORD, help me !' The Syro-
Phenician mother owned herself one of the
despised ones, and the very consciousness of it
made her all the more eager for Christ's notice;
but we deal so much in generalities, that the
true state of our personal condition comes with
very little vividness before us. The Confession
in our Order for Morning and Evening Prayer
is necessarily general, in order to meet the case
of the whole congregation; yet it is often the
limit to our secret acknowledgments of wrong-

doing. We need to be more particular with ourselves, more searching, more honest ; and when we have torn open our secret thoughts, and confessed to ourselves our serious unworthiness, then we may perhaps begin to cry out to Him who alone can improve us, ' LORD, help us !'

Indeed, men have more to do than they are wont to think, to be able to profit by the sacrifice and power of Christ. The Redemption has been provided for all men, but the appropriation of its virtue to each individual soul can only be secured by earnest anxious exertions. If the sin-laden heart is not galled by the weight of sin, if its efforts to release itself are not persistent, if apparent repulses and discouragements are looked upon as insuperable obstacles, then Christ stands before us and we see Him not, or we see Him but feel not His power.

GOD grant us His Holy Spirit, that we may feel the need of crying, ' LORD, help me !' and then ' GOD will help us, and that right early.'

SERMON XVI.

WATCH UNTO PRAYER.

Ascension.

1 St. Peter, iv. 7.

Be ye therefore sober, and watch unto prayer.

Strange words for Simon Peter to use! To him said our Lord in the Garden, 'Simon, sleepest thou? couldest not thou watch one hour? Watch ye and pray, lest ye enter into temptation.' For him, the impetuous, the thoughtlessly self-confident, to say, Be sober, seems a strange contradiction. Well were it for us, if our failures led to a similar recovery. St. Peter speaks his bitter experience, and had felt the mischief of not watching soberly unto prayer: let us too accept the lessons of our experience, and when we fail through infirmity, grow wise for the future.

The words fitly represent the attitude which

the Church should take up at the season of Ascension.

The departure of their loved LORD, with blessing on His lips, with rare promises of succour, of course made a deep impression on the Disciples. As soon as the angels had recalled them to the realities of life, they turned back again to Jerusalem, to ponder over this mysterious event, to take counsel together, and without sitting idle and neglecting the work which seemed now to be opening out before them, to wait and watch unto prayer. 'Not many days hence' was the period fixed for the promise to come; till then they were to watch.

The promised Gift, the Divine Comforter, was to bring them light, to throw into clear relief all the features and bearings of the situation, to explain perplexities, to bring all things to their remembrance whatsoever Christ had said unto them, to shew them things which they understood not at the beginning, to remind them of things which they had unconsciously done to Him in fulfilment of Prophecy, to set their unsettled, bewildered, struggling thoughts at rest. Waiting was the test of their faith! Did they, or did they not, believe His words?

We too have to wait. Holy Scripture foretells many desired and blessed changes, bids us look on towards happy events, as sure to be realized

11

as the coming of the Blessed Spirit; but we
must wait. To us the LORD has bequeathed His
legacy of Peace in reversion, but we must wait.
Peace shall be in the world, when swords shall
be turned into ploughshares, neither shall they
learn war any more. Peace shall be in the
Church, when there shall be one Fold and One
Shepherd. Peace shall be in the soul, when
there shall be joy and peace in believing. But
if these results have not come yet, we must be
sober and watch unto prayer.

Human nature is impatient; we would overleap
all barriers, and plunge at once into the full
transport of enjoyment; just as the soldier prefers
the dash of a sudden assault to the tediousness
of a regular siege. Delay looks to us like defeat,
like sure disappointment. We forget the innumerable obstacles to be surmounted, the countless
circumstances which have to be dove-tailed
together to bring about what we desire. 'Why,'
says the heart to itself, 'why, if GOD's Grace is
almighty, does He not exert sufficient force to
necessitate the end? Why should we have to
wait, when all might be concluded in an
instant?'

Surely, though the Saviour has ascended up
on high, there is enough of His influence left in
the world to sustain our courage for a little
further delay. Why, with such precious gifts
around us, should we avariciously demand the

bestowal of all His store? It is 'the patience of the saints,' that GOD is looking to : He would see what we can bear for His sake, how long we can stay without doubting the sureness of His Word. If we obtained immediate possession of our inheritance, haply, like some spendthrift heir, we should squander all our fortune before we had acquired the tone of character essential to the true enjoyment of our treasure.

I deny not the tryingness of waiting; but in that the real benefit of waiting consists. We fret for peace in the world : and men try, in one way or other, to force the current of the river, and spread the fertilizing waters over tracts so high that the forced stream cannot stay in the upland where they wish it to remain. Some would crush out the violence of nations, and put down war by the sheer force of superior strength. Some would surrender all just grounds of complaint, and buy peace at any cost. Still the world goes on ; still wars and rumours of wars prevail among us. Some even doubt whether the prophecy of final peace through the influence of Christ's Kingdom ever can be realized : and often we wax impatient. Gloomy telegrams from the continent, commercial panics, insurrectionary murmurs, and the clash of actual war, are no proofs of the impossibility of final rest and peace : in GOD's good time good days will come.

So too the members of the Church are saddened

by the lack of unity. Why are Christians broken up into so many various bodies, and animated by such discordant principles? Far off seems the prospect of the 'One Fold, one Shepherd,' being verified. Why does not the LORD hasten the time? Why does not the Blessed Spirit smoothe away the jealousies, misunderstandings, and prejudices, which cause the various branches of the Church to stand aloof,

'Like cliffs that have been rent asunder?'

If Christ's own solemn prayer was that all His might be one, how is His prayer not yet effectual? And so we cherish an unreasonable impatience. The promise is sure: the Unity— and that no false unity, but essential union—will in due course prevail; and as GOD will be all in all, so will the brotherhood and intercommunion of His Children be complete.

Take one other form of impatience. The soul longing for peace finds it not as yet. Christ promised, 'In Me ye shall have peace;' but though we labour and yearn for peace within, it seems coy to us, and turns away. Many an earnest heart is disquieted because it tastes not that joy and peace which are said to accompany believing. Why does not GOD send it? Why cannot I master the cares which distract me? I would fling them off: I hate them with utter loathing, but they refuse to be shaken off: I long to be filled with the love of Christ, but as I have no peace, surely I do not truly love Him.

Oh! indulge not such fretfulness. 'Him that cometh to Me, I will in no wise cast out.'

The remedies to be used are :—

(1.) Be sober. The universe cannot bend itself to your will, therefore look not for too great results. True, the rest of the final restitution of all things, the regeneration when the Son of Man shall sit on the Throne of His Glory, the new heavens and the new earth, are objects worthy of the warmest desire, and in due time will arrive, in spite of all the distress of nations with perplexity, and the discord in the Church, which may now cloud the view; but not one moment sooner than He sees fit Who puts the times and seasons in His own power. Therefore our faithful and happiest course is to go on our appointed way, not wishing to anticipate the end, and not suffering a breath of doubt to darken our hopeful confidence.

(2.) Pray. Our own personal life and peace must ever hang on prayer : only the sense of dependence on GOD will yield us true security. And the final issue may be soon or distant in proportion to the fervour or coldness of our prayers. The only instrument which man possesses for hastening on the triumph of good, the only reliable argument for converting the world, the only channel for peace to ourselves, is prayer.

Therefore, along with sobriety of wish, of act, of word, join constancy of prayer : and at least, it may be said, that, like the refraction of the rising sun, the desired object will be seen before it overtops the horizon—the anticipation of faith will grow almost into a reality.

(3.) Watch unto prayer. How is it that men become disheartened, and cease to pray ? How is it that men fancy their prayers useless ? Because they do not watch the answers to their prayers. The wish is uttered with all earnestness : but it is the convulsive effort of a moment, not sustained, nor followed up. And often the prayer is heard, but the suppliant heeds it not. The answer comes a few moments later than he expected, and his attention is flagging, and he sees it not. Or it comes in a shape for which he asked not, and so the blessing is to him disguised. Yet it is his own blindness ; he should have watched. Watchers see where others notice nothing : their senses are more acute. The prophet's servant on Carmel saw the cloud like a man's hand—Ahab saw nothing.

Sustain we then the voice of prayer to our Ascended LORD, and we shall feel that ' not many days hence ' the promised answer will arrive. But watch the signs of its coming. See you not something more of brotherly kindness between nation and nation ? See you not indications of a desire, a strong desire, for unity in the Church, in the questions now raised as to how near we may approach, Church to Church? And if you closely investigate the dealings of the Spirit with your own heart, you will detect whispers of peace, and find Him blessing your honest endeavours to grow more spiritual, and will find that you have not felt so much peace as you wished, only because you have not noticed the presence of the Spirit of Peace within you. Act on the firm faith that every earnest prayer is heard, and then you will receive insight enough to trace the coming answer. Wait for it, if it comes not at once: it will surely come, it will not tarry. Even where the world would see nothing but unmitigated anger, you will see tenderness. Blows that would crush others will only prove the buoyancy of your faith. Failure in business, beggary, friendlessness, will not prevent your knowing the riches of contentment, and of spiritual blessings. Sudden loss of hearts to which you clung with unutterable affection will not dismay you, nor loosen your hold upon the Love of Christ. You will have grace given you not only to endure, but to believe with unshaken trust, that all the promises of peace will be verified, and that though cast down, though dying, here—rest, strength, life, and joy, shall be yours at last.

SERMON XVII.

LYING.

PROVERBS, XII. 22.

Lying lips are abomination to the LORD.

IT has been truly said, 'Nothing in nature has been so universally decried, and so universally practised withal, as falsehood.' There is something so subtle in the nature of lying, that it, or some of its offshoots, winds its way into the hearts even of wise men, and can only be excluded by most watchful care : for notions of expediency often cloud the conscience, and distort its power of discrimination.

By a 'lie,' I understand speaking contrary to our thoughts, giving utterance to expressions, which misrepresent the feelings—saying one thing, meaning another.

A lie need not be accompanied by words. We may act a lie, when we do things to mislead others and throw them off the scent.

On the other hand, it is possible to speak against truth and yet not lie, provided we speak in good faith. 'There is one that slippeth in his speech, but not from his heart.' It is speaking in bad faith, with conscious purpose of deceiving, that is a lie. For instance, if you say, 'The man is not here,' though he may actually be, it is no lie, if you believe that he is not.

I shall not enter into the question whether there may not be exceptional cases—cases in which it is difficult to say how far we may be justified in making a false statement, in order to prevent some grievous wrong or injury being done—but I will take the text on the broad general ground that lying is abomination to the LORD.

To discover the heinousness of lying, we need search no further than the third chapter of Genesis. What brought sin and misery upon our race? What was the first step in the Temptation of the Serpent? a lie insinuated with plausible kindness, and predictions of supposed benefit: 'Ye shall be as Gods.' Most truly did our LORD say of Satan, 'He is a liar, and the father of it:' and we have good cause to look with horror on that which was the immediate cause of so much ruin to us.

Again, the First, Second, Third, and Ninth, Commandments of the Decalogue are directed against some form of falsehood—false gods, false

worship, false application of the NAME of the GOD
of Truth, false witness.

And in the vision of the final condition of the
human race it is proclaimed, 'All liars shall have
their part in the lake which burneth with fire and
brimstone :' and again, 'without (the city) are
dogs, and sorcerers, and whoremongers, and
murderers, and idolaters, and (found in goodly company forsooth!) whosoever loveth and maketh a lie.'

It scarcely needs to subjoin examples to enhance
the loathing which Holy Scripture seeks to rouse
against this sin, by mentioning the old prophet
of Bethel, Ananias and Sapphira, and Judas,
with his acted lie—'Master, is it I?' 'Hail
Master! and kissed Him.'

Now take the word in its honest downright
form : do not let us shelter ourselves under smooth
expressions—equivocation, prevarication, dissem-
bling, simulation, untruthfulness—longer words,
by which men try to take the edge from unpleasant
facts—but which all in the end point to the same
thing, a want of sincerity. And whatever you
may do to soften off the epithet and description,
there remains the text in all its decision and
boldness—'Lying lips *are* abomination to the
LORD,' and lying lips must hereafter become
despairing and miserable lips, when the truth shall
force itself through them, and they shall open to
disclose gnashing teeth, in the fire which never
shall be quenched.

Nor is the verdict of man less decisive. Even while they practise it, men condemn lying. Perjury is a crime branded by all governments, heathen as well as Christian. One of the three essentials of the Persian education was to teach a child to speak the truth; and in every well-conducted school the moral offence of lying is detested and sharply punished.

Look at it also in this light. We apply the word 'true' to all that is good and worthy. Is it not our instinctive feeling that truth is the object most worthy of attaining? Do not so-called philosophers profess to aim at truth? Is it not our conception of GOD formed under a sense that He is Truth itself? Do we not call the Gospel, the good news of salvation, the Truth?

Its opposite, then, must be proportionately odious: and so we learn to execrate everything that savours of falsehood or deceit: and if men search for a cutting epithet in their passion, is not one of the first they think of, the word 'liar?'

Reflect also on the mischief which lying occasions to society. It is by mutual confidence, by faith in the honesty and purity of each other's motives, that we live on together. No peace can be where there is no trust. If a despot has no peace, it is because his conscience tells him that he has cause to fear treachery: and if some left-handed Ehud comes with deceitful words, 'I have a message from GOD unto thee,' he would most likely feel suspicious of the design. And how would trade or business be carried on, where there was no credit, no trust in a man's word? and credit cannot be, where there is no truthfulness. You trust not, whom you suspect.

The mischief produced by a lie is incalculable. One deliberate slander may blast a man's character for life, may endanger his safety. It was by spreading and working upon false rumours of sedition, that Nero obtained the applause of the Roman populace for burning and torturing Christians.

No doubt the lie often recoils; as on Gehazi's body, while he persisted to Elisha that he 'went no whither,' there started up the instantaneous leprosy, and upon Ananias and his wife there fell the speedy judgment of death. Yet the mischief remains.

That falsehood should pass away, and men should live in perfect good faith and sincerity, every man speaking the truth with his neighbour, is a state of things, which to some seems Utopian and impossible—perhaps it may be—yet it should be the object of our devoutest wish. 'Who shall dwell in Thy Tabernacle? .... he .... that speaketh the truth from his heart.' Heaven is full of truth, and only if Heaven be an impossibility can it be impossible to conceive the prevalence of truth. May it come, and speedily!

Now every age has its own style of vice and

sin. Let us see some of the sort of lies which prevail now-a-days.

1. White lies, as they are called—lies which are glossed over and decorated by fashion—specious habits of talk, and conventional phrases ; justified by necessity, expediency, or the like ; or because understood by all not to be meant, therefore warrantable. So the world says : but I cannot see any justification in what people choose to call expediency—that is, expediency framed upon your own wishes. If you set your heart on some unlawful object, which you are sure that you cannot attain by going straight at it, are you justified in reaching it by a crooked path ? Can you cheat your conscience ? After a time, you can even do that : but at first—before the hot iron has seared it—your conscience will not be quieted by the argument that the end justifies the means, and that if the end is innocent, a dishonest mode of procuring it is not evil. Some minds are very subtle in drawing distinctions, when it serves their turn ; but it is not so easy to substantiate them.

2. Slander.—This is not peculiar to our age—witness the cases of Mephibosheth, Naboth, Jeremiah, the Blessed LORD Himself, all victims of false accusation—but it is not rare in our age. Whether it is some supposed interest which the slanderer fancies he has in traducing the character of an innocent rival ; or whether it is a morbid

and miserable pleasure in seeing the fall of another; or the love of shewing power, even at the expense of a neighbour; it is equally odious, and an act of which a heathen, not to say a Christian, should be thoroughly ashamed.

3. Lies to screen our faults.——These are more natural and intelligible. To escape the consequences of a sin by hiding it, seems a tangible advantage; but is it? Do we gain by cloking one fault with another?

> ' Nothing can need a lie ;
> A fault which needs one most, grows two thereby.'
>
> *G. Herbert.*

Gehazi may do it, but he loses by the act. And every right-minded man would have a thousand times more pity for one who owned his fault and asked forgiveness, than for one who tried to elude detection. There is a baseness, a meanness, in a lie, which stifles all one's compassion, and rouses all one's anger, when it is detected; for it seems to say, 'I could not trust you, knowing how I had offended you, to be at all lenient or forgiving, and so I thought I would keep you in the dark, and run my chance of detection: and this is galling to one's self-respect, as if we were considered incapable of self-control and justice. We can find a sort of sympathy, at all events a pity, for the ruins of a man's noble qualities, when he comes to us sorrowing over them, and humbled to the dust by a sense of his error, and throwing himself on our compassion, appeals to our superiority and leniency; but we are disgusted with one who has no self-respect, and no respect for us, who in using a lie deems us simple enough to be cajoled, and considers the doubling of his sin preferable to owning himself in the wrong.

This is said of sins against our fellow-men: how much more forcibly it applies to sins against GOD! In their folly men sometimes imagine that they can escape His searching glance; that with their heart crowded with sinful projects and false intentions, they can enter in with smoothed and innocent face, and stand before their Master, with a 'GOD, I thank Thee that I am not as other men are!' One would fain hope that such self-deception is rare; yet it were well to remember that pardon can only await the penitent heart, which humbly confesses its offence. If you would secure forgiveness for the faults of which your conscience is afraid, make an unreserved and undisguising confession. Out with it all! Start not back because the sin looks so ugly, so unpardonable; instead of palliating it or excusing it, make the worst of it; you cannot lose by so doing, for GOD will never condemn you more than you deserve; but you will gain, by a deepening hatred of sin, and a lower, truer, humility. Try to soften down your fault, and His forgiveness will not flow so freely; own that your life hangs on His Mercy, and He will veil His Majesty : justify yourself, and His Majesty will stand out alone in its sternest, most relentless, justice.

4. Two other modes of lying frequently cross my own path of life.

(*a.*) In asking for relief, (I trust there are none here of this class, but it is common enough,) there are some who simulate and exaggerate their poverty to move the hearts of the charitable. They let their home look wretched and squalid, garnish it with rags and unsightly dirt, and so impose upon those who cannot search the heart and lay bare the falsehood. Those acquainted with the poor well know that where there is no cleanliness there is little worthiness, and that often and often there is far more real need of assistance (and of course infinitely more deserving,) where all looks neat and clean : and will therefore endeavour to help most, where neatness and cleanliness are to be found. But it is fitting that they, who make up tales of misery to entrap the unwary, should be warned how grievously they offend Almighty GOD, by Whose ears lying lips cannot but be heard, and to Whom they are an abomination, which must finally be punished. 'A lying tongue is but for a moment.'

(*b.*) In the publication of the Banns of Marriage, false addresses are frequently given, and that with an assurance perfectly startling. It is done with deliberate particularity ; the number of the house, the street, the room, specified falsely, while the parties live in a totally different parish. I do not know what sort of a conscience a clergyman is supposed to have, to wink at such things. And all this is done by otherwise respectable people, to avoid publicity! There is nothing to be ashamed of in marriage, which is 'honourable among all men,' a holy dignified estate : and it is very false and sinful modesty, which would hide itself under cover of a lie ; and very poor policy which would commence a new condition of life, with a big lie as the first step in it—in other words, with the curse of Him to Whom 'lying lips are abomination.'

But on the whole. Let us see to the truthfulness of our hearts and lips. If we are children of GOD, members of Christ, temples of the Holy Ghost, we must be truthful. If we can bear to tell a lie, we know whose children we are—not GOD's, but ——

If there is such a thing as truth, for which Christ died, of which He came to bear witness, into which the Holy Ghost leads us ; then the faintest breath of falsehood must be a hateful, poisonous, scorching blast, which we cannot face. All is clear and open in Heaven : all is dark, disguised, crooked, perverted, in Hell.

Oh ! if you are tempted to utter words of deceit, remember how abominable such things are to the LORD, and how they bar up impenetrably

12

the gates of Heaven, which fly open at the approach of truth.   Pray we that He Who is Truth would keep our tongues from 'evil speaking, lying, and slandering,' and make us to take pleasure in speaking the truth from our hearts; that so we may not be ashamed when we stand face to face with GOD, but with all our infirmities, all our transgressions, we may have the solid comfort of being unconscious of insincerity, honest in purpose and word, however unsuccessful in deed; true in heart, true in speech; true to ourselves, true to our GOD: and so may realize the truth of His Promise, Who never lies, that those who seek His Truth shall find it complete on His Heavenly Throne.

SERMON XVIII.

SOW IN TEARS.

PSALM CXXVI. 5.

They that sow in tears, shall reap in joy.

THE occasion which called forth this Psalm is doubtful.

Was it a song of triumph at the defeat of Sennacherib, and the miraculous annihilation of his army? 'Then were we like unto them that dream,' might well be said at that time, for 'when they arose early in the morning, behold! they (their foes) were all dead corpses.'

Or was it rather the utterance of those restored from captivity in Babylon? We know how the exiled Jews mourned. Nehemiah for sorrow of heart could scarce pour forth the wine for Artaxerxes. Daniel opened the window of his chamber which faced in the direction of Jerusalem, which he longed to see. Jeremiah and

Ezekiel lamented over the fall of their country. Their Home, their City, their Temple, they all yearned after. What was dignity, honour, wealth, among aliens, without their fatherland, the Land of Promise?

Proportionate to the pining desire for home was the joy of the Jews at their restoration. 'Then were we like unto them that dream; .... the LORD hath done great things for us.' 'Turn our captivity as the rivers in the south;' that is, 'as the torrent-bed is dry in summer but replenished as winter draws on, so let our dry, empty, cheerless, blank, captivity be converted into the rich associations and joys of home again.'

'They that sow in tears shall reap in joy.' 'By the waters of Babylon we sat down and wept.' 'Mine eye runneth down with rivers of water.' 'Oh! that my head were waters, and mine eyes a fountain of tears.'—But they 'reaped in joy,' when in GOD's Providence they were allowed once again to see their native country.

But I would adopt a general view of the text.

1. 'Sow in tears.' 'In tears' means 'in time of tears,' not 'sow tears.'

And why should I enlarge upon the prevalence of afflictions?

> 'Tears from the birth the doom must be
> Of the sin-born.'
>
> (*Lyra Innocentium.*)

Who so fortunate as to escape troubles in life? The rich? Riches are themselves a care. The healthy? Health will not save from anxiety: loss of estate may come to the healthy, or slander, or disappointment, or misunderstanding. The good-tempered or contented? Ill health, poverty, may be theirs: they cannot help giving offence to some.

We all think we know what tears are, and troubles: all, that we know more than others about vexation; and naturally, because our own troubles are our own, and 'the heart knoweth his own bitterness,' and it comes close up to our heart, and hugs it: and what frettings go on in our secret breast the world does not see.

But it is the way of taking troubles that is the thing to consider; and we may speak to each other, and help each other, in this matter.

The Psalm says 'they who *sow in tears*.' What does this mean?

Tears in the moral world answer to heavy rains in the natural world. The soil is saturated, unfit for sowing: but if the husbandman sows no seed, because the seed-time is unpropitious, harvest he can have none. 'Blessed are ye that sow beside all waters.' 'He that regardeth the wind shall not sow.'

So in the moral world. Distresses thicken over us; floods of sorrow spread over our work, our hopes; clouds darken our bright sky; but still, we must sow, sow the good seed of 'faith, hope, and charity,' the seed of 'patient waiting for Christ,' the seed of 'holiness, without which no man shall see the LORD.'

Now consider, how the world behaves itself in tears—in time of sorrows.

Suppose the sorrows come outwardly.

Israel had lost Joseph; Simeon was a captive; and the Egyptian lord had sent to fetch away his Benjamin. 'All these things are against me.' In his murmuring he quite forgat the mercies, which GOD had showered on him: they were to go for nothing! only his troubles he would nurse and brood over! There are many like him among us. There comes a big sorrow—we lose a very dear one, the light of our eyes, the joy of our heart: the blank caused by our bereavement seems irreparable, we stare vacantly into the air, refusing to be comforted, we harbour bitter thoughts of GOD, and call Him in our hearts cruel and severe.

Or a man is pinched for food. Trade has been so dull, that for weeks in the inclement winter he has failed to procure work; he feels sharp hunger himself, he sees his wife and children famishing, and a kind of madness seizes him. The time of tears is upon him; or rather, his heart aches and boils so that he cannot cry; tears would have softened and soothed him—a low murmur gradually swells out into open reproaches; perhaps it is the employer he blames, or the cold-hearted rich, or even the loving Father above!

But in neither of these two instances does the man *sow* in his tears. Could he bring himself to do this, he would soon reap in joy. The bereaved one would try to be patient, call to mind ancient mercies, think of mercies still remaining, try to dwell on the blessings of spiritual duties, to feed on the love of GOD, would take out his Bible, search for comfort and antidotes to grief, pour out his heart-aches to Him who knows them, has permitted them, can sanctify them to him. That is the seed for him to sow: such seed might not spring up at once, but it would not fail to bear joyful fruit in time.

So also, the man in distress would strive to believe that in spite of temporary poverty there remained a good hope of getting on better presently: he would have recourse to a store-house which never fails, where bread is laid up for everyone that seeks it. 'Man doth not live by bread alone.' He would not lean on human assistance alone, from charitable funds, or trades unions. These may be needful in their way, in some respects: but only trust in GOD will really break the neck of the affliction. If he can but grasp the nourishing power of the Bread of Life, he has found out the secret of life, the principle by which man lives, *viz.* by the Will of GOD.

This is the true seed to sow. Do we sow it, when we are in tears?

Or again. Tears may imply sins, or temptations to sin. Many hours of sadness are caused by a feeling of sin. There is none of us without sin—woe betide us, if we think we are! Each knows best what his besetting sin is, and its frightful pertinacious power. In some, this consciousness has the effect of freezing all exertion: the temptation seems to steal upon them like a numbing frost; they see its onward approach, and know its fatal influence, but cannot rouse themselves. Of what use to warn them? 'I know my danger,' says the victim, 'I know that my sin has fastened its deadly fangs in my soul; but I cannot get rid of it. Why should I struggle? I am none the better for it! Plague me not with your well-meant advice; you do not understand me.' What! is that the strain, in which the farmer is to cry out, when the rains are excessive? 'My labour is thrown away, I give it up in despair.' He would not do so: he sows his seed; it may not all mature, but some will. So, you may not eradicate a vicious habit by one effort; you may not subdue your temper by a mere exercise of will: the coils of the Serpent Tempter wind round and round, and patiently and courageously must you unwind them joint by joint: but *let* the loathsome brute twine itself and fix its venom in your limbs! no,

never, without an endeavour to tear yourself
free. And *let* a sinful habit remain, without
battling with it, though you know, if it masters
you, it will destroy your soul! No, no, Brethren!
Here is GOD's grace freely at your command;
all needful power He offers you, you have but
to exert it. Sow the seed, the good seed. Plant
the seed—that is, repent. Water the seed—that
is, amend. By your belief in GOD, wait for the
increase. In tears sow: amid sins practise faith
and good works: out of sins struggle amain, and
you shall reap in joy—that is, your sins shall part
from you, shall be buried out of GOD's sight, and
gradually be lost to *your* view; and for your
repentance you shall find joy. It was a heavy
trial time, when you were sowing: it shall be a
joyous time, when you are reaping. 'Blessed are
they that mourn, for they shall be comforted.'
The seed of faith shall grow, the fruit of holiness
shall be reaped: what you prized most when you
smarted under sin, you shall prize most now that
you have conquered sin: you valued it when days
were dark; the days shall be bright and yet you
shall value it still.

But what we need most is faith to sow.
Anxieties often so fluster us, that we omit to
make GOD our refuge; and because all earthly
refuges fail us, therefore we lose heart. But
there is no call for it. Lose heart! when the
Almighty GOD has promised to help you! That

were folly indeed. Learn rather to measure
things as they are, not as you in thoughtlessness
fancy them. It is a shame that there should be
courage enough where physical courage is needed,
but such timidity when we are struggling for the
soul's life. Many a man could plunge bravely
and unhesitatingly into the freezing water, as
the treacherous ice cracked and engulphed the
shrieking crowd. Danger was defied, in hope of
rescuing some fellow-creature ; and men trusted
to a strong arm, and firm grasp of the rope, and
the swimmer's bold stroke, and bragged not of it
afterwards. But here are we, with our souls and
the souls of others in jeopardy, ready to exclaim,
'It's all hopeless : my natural temper is never
to be conquered.' Oh ! is hell so passable and
tolerable in its horrors, that you can bear to
speak so coolly about it ? Is Heaven so in-
differently pleasant, that you can let it slip
from your grasp without anything more than a
sigh ?

Remember, here is a promise, 'shall reap in
joy.' It is a right noble and solid joy which the
husbandman feels, when he reaps the good corn
and houses it safely. Amply then is all his toil
repaid. Thankful is he that he did not observe
the wind, nor regard the cloud, but in spite of all
threatening weather sowed his seed. He has his
reward. And shall not we—if we love GOD
through all our trials, temptations, sorrows, tears ;

if we serve Him, trust Him, through all; if we live holy lives in the fear of GOD, regarding His Will as our highest law;—shall not we have our reward?

Let the world scoff. Let fools ridicule the smallness of the seed, the slowness of its growth. Never mind: we may sow in tears, amid insults and scorn; but if in tears we *sow*, we shall reap in joy; reap peace in our hearts, and bliss in Heaven.

SERMON XIX.

THE LORD'S DAY.

GENESIS, II. 3.

And GOD *blessed the seventh day and sanctified
it.*

THE Sunday question naturally attracts much
attention, for it is a very practical question,
seeing that so much of our comfort and ease is
bound up with it, and that the measure of its
obligation is so much discussed. Whether we
speak of Sunday, the Sabbath, or the LORD'S
Day, we mean a day of *rest,* as the name Sabbath
implies.

Moreover, the fact that one nation for centuries
observed the Sabbath, and that all Christendom
has from the first observed the LORD'S Day, is
something more than a coincidence.

1. The origin of a rest-day we trace to the
time denoted in the text. It was ordained by

GOD Himself, not in connection with the Jewish people only, but before they were formed into a nation. And the text furnishes a *principle* to be followed by us, *viz.* the duty of devoting a certain portion of our time to rest, because GOD rested.

2. Later on in Scripture history we find the Jewish Sabbath enforced for a double reason, (*a*) Exodus, xx. 11, because GOD rested from creation, and (*b*) Deut. v. 15, because the Israelites had rest from their slave work in Egypt on the seventh day. This ordinance was one of the distinguishing marks of the Jewish Church : and special stress is laid upon it throughout the Law and the Prophets.

3. How did our LORD deal with it? To the Pharisees He asserted His right as Son of Man to interpret, regulate, or overrule, its observance— 'The Son of Man is LORD also of the Sabbath;' and then declared the principle, that as 'the Sabbath was made for man,' necessity or charity were to override positive enactments, and the letter of the Law was to yield to the exigencies of man; as for example, when ears of corn were plucked to appease hunger, or the sick healed in extremity. Consequently, even to the Jew the Sabbath was not an arbitrary law, but a provision designed for his benefit. And we ourselves may learn from this instance, how by too rigid adherence to the letter we may sometimes altogether miss the spirit of a law.

**4. How did the Apostles, expounding Christ's
Will, and instructed by Him, act?** Like their
Master, being born under the Jewish Law,
they observed the Sabbath, by going into the
synagogue, and joining in the public worship,
on that sacred day. But as regarded the Gentile
Christians, they did not enjoin observance of the
Sabbath. At the first Council in Jerusalem, the
keeping of the Sabbath was not reckoned among
the few things required of the Gentiles. And
St. Paul (Col. ii. 16.) speaking to Gentiles
specially, (and be it remembered that we are of
the Gentiles,) says, 'Let no man *judge* you in
meat or drink, or in respect of an holy-day, or of
the new moon, or of the *Sabbath* days, which are
a shadow of things to come, but the body is
Christ;' *i. e.* the Gentile Christians were not to
be condemned for non-observance of the Jewish
Sabbath : in other words, the Sabbath as observed
by the Jews was abolished.

But we find *a* day observed by the Apostles
and Gentile Christians, *viz.* the LORD's Day,
Christ's Day, Who then rested from the work
of Redemption. It was on this first day of the
week that the disciples met together to break
bread at Troas. St. Paul bids the Corinthians
lay by their offerings on the first day of the
week. St. John speaks of being in the Spirit on
the LORD's Day.

In point of fact, the Jewish Christians observed

both the Sabbath and the LORD'S Day : but the Church did not require the Gentile converts to keep the Sabbath, which gradually fell into the shade till the LORD'S Day stood alone as the weekly rest.

We may therefore consider the observance of the first or LORD'S Day to be binding on us. In what sense, it may be asked, do we then acknowledge the Fourth Commandment?

Referring to the original institution of the rest-day, we find set forth the principle of dedicating one seventh part of our time to GOD; and therefore in principle, whether that part be the first day or seventh day in *order* makes no matter : and if we keep one day in seven, we obey the Fourth Commandment.

Hence the due observance of Sunday is obligatory on the Christian—

(1) Because a rest was enjoined at Creation by GOD, and has not been canceled since :

(2) Because the Church, as shewn in the practice of the Apostles and early Christians, appointed the observance of the LORD'S Day—a canon, which the Apostles, being inspired, were perfectly competent to frame :

(3) Because profitable to man.

Now what is the nature of the LORD'S Day Rest? Jehovah's rest was of course not from weariness, but as a symbol and example for our sakes, that we might keep a rest which *is* needful for us. Besides, His Rest indicates a spiritual rest; for He still works, 'My Father worketh hitherto;' He never ceases the work of regulating the world, sustaining His creatures. 'There remaineth therefore a rest for the people of GOD.' And this point will materially help us to understand the true Sunday rest. But (1) our Sunday rest *is* to be a bodily rest notwithstanding. Nature tells us our need of bodily repose. Sleep is essential to the recruiting of our tired faculties : nothing is more exhausting than sleeplessness : broken rest is the cause of many a pale and haggard face and drooping frame. And I ask any hard-working man or woman—whether artizan or statesman, man of business or labourer, needle-woman or authoress, or lady superintendent—what would be the result to our bodily health, if we were deprived of Sunday rest? Nay, it is an acknowledged feeling : for not only so, but men are clamouring and agitating, as never before, for half-holidays, and short hours—I am not sure that they do not go too far in their demands—and all this proves that men feel the need of cessation from work. Our very beasts of burden need it : a horse cannot work seven days continuously without being exhausted. What coachman would think of working his team so ? Much more do we, who have not only the strain of bodily powers, but mental exertions and anxieties superadded, need a pause from time to time, that we may repair the loss of vigour. Surely the Church is more than justified in calling on all employers of labour to facilitate. as much as possible the setting apart of a day sacred to rest, and on the public generally not to imagine that such persons as cabmen, railway guards, and keepers of places of recreation, stand in no need of their rest.

But now what sort of bodily rest befits the LORD'S Day? Is it sleeping? Though sleep is a necessary part of rest, it should not engross all our time : excessive sleep would not recruit but enervate the body. Feasting or merriment? On the same ground, this in excess tires rather than rests. If you consider Sunday a suitable day for festive gaiety and excursions, you surely misunderstand its rest. There may be a quiet relaxation without boisterous mirth, whereas boisterous mirth is often not only fatiguing, but accompanied with unseemly language and misconduct. And when it is considered that the Rest-day is appointed by GOD, any conduct which would displease Him must be inconsistent with a due observance of Sunday. There are many ways of innocent, rational, and seemly, refreshment of body; and these are legitimate. It is quite as much contrary to the spirit of the seventh day's rest to forbid the enjoyment of the outward beauties and attractions of nature, as

13

to launch out into extravagant excitement and festivity. On the LORD's Day His works are a fitting object of contemplation and wholesome source of delight: and to forbid the weary mechanic, or the exhausted thinker, to spend any time in gazing on bright skies, while the soft fresh air bathes his hot temples, is a prudery akin to insanity. Let the worn-out workers refresh themselves with air and exercise, only let them not spend all their holy-day in such pastime, nor in excess of mere animal enjoyment.

2. But the rest should be spiritual too: for I am addressing those who profess to care for their souls, and not the simply ungodly. The true aim of the LORD's Day is to give us respite from the whirl and din of the world, to provide a breathing space, in which to dismiss cares and anxieties. The mind gives way before anxiety, if it be not sometimes interrupted. Our madhouses are peopled with those whose overwrought brain has worn itself out. Our true life cannot be sustained except by banishing such worrying seeds of distraction. We have a spiritual work to do, from which the world drags us back. Toil, pleasure, care, unfit us for it. We want leisure to think of it, to cultivate it. In the Rest-day we have an admirable opportunity; we need not work, nor pursue earthly studies, for they may be laid by without attracting even the

world's notice; and we may set ourselves to higher pursuits, the food of our souls, the growth of our spiritual being.

You may say, We may do this at all times. True : but will you ? Any time is no time. Fix a time, and you deprive your vacillating mind of one main aid of self-deception. He who thinks that any time is fit for prayer is in danger of omitting prayer altogether : the habit recalls the desire and the spirit for prayer. A definite time brings a definite purpose and method. ' I'll do it some day or other' means nothing : we can only bring ourselves to the point by fixing a period. If method is needed in households, workshops, and common business, much more in spiritual work.

Hence one way of profitably spending part of this day is in defined and systematic public worship.

It is often asked, Why so much stress is laid on Church-going, when we can pray and read the Holy Scriptures, and, in these days at least, a sermon also, at home ? I ask, in return, Do men, who do not go to Church, take the trouble to think for themselves—to entertain spiritual thoughts—to work out their own salvation ? In nine cases out of ten, the time of the absentees is spent in something unprofitable or worse. Public worship is a public test of our loyalty to Christ, of our concern for our soul. True, Church-going is not infallibly attended with heart-worship, but absence from Church is much oftener associated with unspiritual life. It is good to commit ourselves in the service of GOD. If we make a point of paying this homage, and seeking the aids and opportunities of the public assembly of the Church, we shall not be without special profit.

Hold fast the LORD's Day as a precious heirloom, suiting all times. An ill day will it be for us when it shall be abolished; and all glory be to GOD for His Providence in instituting it!

And oh! if you would enjoy the Sabbath promised to the faithful in Heaven, seek to improve the Sabbath on earth. We must practise ourselves for Heaven, by realizing spiritual rest in this life. Make your Sundays periods of holy rest and refreshment for your souls, and then you will not only be refreshed for more vigorous work in your daily occupation, but, by spiritual refreshment drawn from the Life of Christ, be prepared for His Presence hereafter.

SERMON XX.

THE CHRISTIAN'S CROSS.

St. Mark, x. 21.

Come, take up the cross.

Some graces have a special attractiveness. One of these is fervour. In presence of an enthusiastic person you feel fired and infected with the same spirit, you wonder perhaps how you could have been so cold, and you grow ashamed of your former lukewarmness.

Our Blessed Lord was touched with the sight of ardent emotions. On one occasion, as He went forth on His road, and met a young man running breathless up to Him, with an eager earnest question, 'What shall I do to inherit eternal life?' His heart warmed towards him, and 'beholding him He loved him.'

Certainly zeal is far more loveable than cold calculating. Its freshness, its buoyancy, its look of youthfulness, is most engaging, especially to those who have experienced the dry, cautious, heartless, dealing of the world.

Yet warmth of feeling is liable to mislead. It may suggest to a man the idea, 'Because I am sincere, in earnest, and ready to act, therefore I must be right in the course which I have adopted.' Fervour may go hand in hand with impatience, anger, sharpness of tone. Enthusiasts are not always the pleasantest people to deal with, nor always trustworthy, because they see with biased eyes, and do not weigh the general bearings of any case.

And there is mostly lacking in such a character just that point which was lacking in the young man who came so hurriedly and ardently to our LORD—patience. Do anything for Christ! what would he not do? what was too arduous? Should he go to the desert, like John the Baptist, and preach? He would go. Should he risk his life in nursing the sick and plague-stricken? He would do it. Should he spend days and nights in the Temple, or the synagogue, or pray whole nights on the chilly mountain? He would do it. But our LORD asked not for that; for He says, 'Come, take up the cross.' It was comparatively easy to make exertions in the direction which the man's own bent indicated, but more than he could bear to follow a course against his will. Commandment after Commandment is enumerated, and he eagerly exclaims, 'I have kept it;' but at last the weak point in his mind is touched, 'Go and sell that thou hast, and give to the poor, and come, take up the cross.' If he kept his riches, he could do many things condescendingly, without injury to his pride, or interference with his will. But the pinch is, and this he felt at once, when we are to do or submit, where we fret to do and submit. It is irksome to take up the cross.

The phrase 'Take up the cross,' implies the carrying the instrument of one's own shame or misery, and contains an allusion to felons being compelled to bear their cross to the place of execution. Many of us would prefer dying on the cross to carrying the cross. It is easier to support the piercing sharpness of a death agony, though the pain at the moment be intense, than to put up with, and carry about, the disgrace, the shame, the dull tediousness, of a constant fretting. 'Take up the cross,' implies incessant, daily, submission to ignominy, persecution, annoyance. The LORD, as He went up the Hill of Scorn, dragged along roughly and unfeelingly, while jeers and taunts and blasphemy were flung upon Him, was bearing His Cross. That slow torture was perhaps more agonizing to His sensitive mind than the scourging or the piercing of the nails. For some great calamity men seem to gather supernatural strength: they collect their whole energies, and every nerve is strained for enduring. Weak and timid people can prepare their minds to face a severe operation, or to battle with a terrible sorrow; even they can stand the shock of a sudden bereavement, can bear to be stripped of every earthly solace for a time; but the continual putting up with perhaps lesser, but incessantly teazing annoyances, is even to bolder spirits intolerable. Yet Christ says, ' Come, take up the cross.'

Again consider another instance in this same chapter. James and John asked for high place at Christ's right and left hand. Possibly they did not at all understand that His career would be otherwise than a victorious progress, and a rapid exaltation to an earthly monarchy: but, even if they counted upon an arduous struggle, the sort of conflict they did not thoroughly realize. They were prepared, they thought, to dare anything for their LORD—the event proved them equal to their anticipations; for James, through the Grace of GOD, bowed his neck to the sword of Herod, and John bare himself bravely before the persecutors of the Cross—but I doubt whether at this time they felt in what the bitterness of the cup chiefly consisted, which He called upon them to drink—not in the pangs of wounds and bodily tortures, but in the mental struggle with sin, the daily lifelong cross, such as St. John bore in Patmos.

When our LORD therefore spoke of the cross,

it was of that constant, dragging, trying, contest, which most of us must have felt, and some very keenly, between our own inclinations or comfort, and the worries and anxieties of life. Whence they come, it matters not: whether from overt injuries or slander, or from fancied wrongs, whether from others' roughness and spite, or from our own sensitiveness: there they hang, like a heavy vapour shrouding us round and veiling the sunlight. These are the sort of things which make the cross. Each has his own. One is scorned by some proud neighbour, another slandered: a parent finds his child rebellious, a servant is misunderstood by her mistress—a slight, a misconstruction, a daily persecution, or misinterpretation of motives—these are more galling by far than bodily pains. Worldly ruin is not so overwhelming, a fierce crushing disaster (so crushing that it seems to have reached the limit of heaviness, and as if nothing worse *could* happen,) is trifling to the constant fretting of little anxieties: a broken limb, a violent fever, are comparatively easy to surmount; but the wear, the tedious aching pressure, of some habitual anxiety, is so hard to bear, like the sense of sinking which accompanies the debility of a weakened constitution.

'How are we to bear this? Tell us some cure, (you will say)—none so eager to escape it as we who feel it—but how to bear the cross?'

Note the words of the text.

1. 'Come.' Our dear LORD invites us to Himself. He does not stand and haughtily bid us go and bear it. He does not chide us for foolishly caring about these things. He does not speak sharply, but calls and beckons us to His side, Himself to lay upon us the cross which is to gall us, in love for us, that we may profit by the discipline. The myrtle leaf gives out more fragrance by being bruised: and the branches of the True Vine must be made a sweet savour unto GOD by suffering. Christ is willing to listen to our complaints, to hear all our feelings poured into His patient ear, to explain His own strength and love, that we may be encouraged to submit patiently, resting on His grace to help us. Where we have some One ready to enter into all our disquietude, without flinging us back in scorn, half the battle is over, and our courage is re-animated.

2. 'Take up the cross.' We are deliberately to place it on ourselves, and endure it. We had better not try to procure others to bear it with us, or for us, but set *ourselves* to exertion. If others bear it, it is not ours, it does us no good. When you have a perplexity, and know not which way to turn, each path seeming to have great drawbacks, you would like someone to take the responsibility of directing your course: but it is not good for you to pin your judgment on

another's opinion. It is right to ask guidance from those who are fit or authorized to guide, but a good guide will not tell you exactly what to do, but rather give rules and principles, which you must use and apply for yourself. Your cross lies before you; you are summoned to take it up. Do not hesitate. It looks rough and heavy, too heavy;—as Cain said of his punishment, 'greater than I can bear;'—but you are to strive to bear it: begin to lift it, and your strength will seem to come to you. Take it up cheerfully, in faith that He Who bids you do it will nerve you to support the weight.

3. 'Follow ME.' Christ has carried His Cross before us. What a cross is, who knows so well as He? How to carry it, who knows so well as He? How to help you to carry it, who knows so well as He? You need not be reluctant, when He invites, Who is the Great Physician, the tender Sympathizer, the powerful Advocate.

And after all, look steadily at the cross. Many pretty and holy fancies have been twined round the cross—its form, its look, its position—but look at the realities which vex your soul, take the measure of your cares, contrast them with what you would think smooth and pleasant. I grant them bitter, heavy, harassing, at the time; but if they are borne, and patiently received, for Christ's sake, then you soon learn to look back on them with thankfulness: they had a poisonous taste, but their power was needed for the disease, and the constitution has been benefited by them. Martha had cares: Jesus taught her to bear them, and we find her spiritual life much strengthened at the death of her brother. Job had troubles, crushing and countless troubles; but his sorrows taught him to 'let patience have her perfect work,' and his gratitude was warmly expressed afterwards. What perfected saint but looks back gratefully to sorrow, which the grace of GOD helped him to bear? Take up *your* cross.

SERMON XXI.

FREE-WILL.

DEUTERONOMY, V. 29.

O that there were such an heart in them, that they would fear Me, and keep all My Commandments always, that it might be well with them, and with their children for ever!

THERE is no doubt a broad distinction between the Old Testament and New Testament Scriptures, the Law and the Gospel; but many press too heavily upon it: and we should not forget that the source of both is the same: from the same Holy Spirit flows the inspiration which breathes through all the Canonical Books.

It is of vital importance to believe in the inspiration of the Old Testament.

If the Old Testament be rejected as not of Divine origin, many strong evidences in favour of our LORD's claims to our worship are lost.

For example, the prophecies so minutely fulfilled in the Person of Jesus Christ, the account of the origin of sin, and of the necessity of its expiation by blood, the ancient wistful desires of holy men for the Redemption which they all felt needed, all which the Old Testament records—these materially strengthen the position which our LORD occupies now as the Saviour promised long, for Whose coming the world was prepared by continuous discipline.

Besides, if Christ is the eternal Son of GOD, He is such as St. John describes : ' In the beginning was the WORD, ... and the WORD was GOD.' And it is a convincing corroboration of this point, if it can be shewn that the same character and attributes, which He claims and possesses in the story of the Gospels, are claimed and possessed by Jehovah in the Old Testament Scriptures.

Now if the Gospels teach us anything, they teach us that GOD is Love. The coming of the Son of GOD to suffer for man, the infinite pains taken by Him to convince, persuade, draw, men to Himself, by example and precept and self-devotion, put in the richest but truest colours the unspeakable mercy of GOD, Who could so interest Himself in behalf of those who had rejected Him.

But the older Scriptures, if we read them carefully, are not of a different spirit. Some would treat the Old Testament as describing an obsolete worn-out system, which places GOD in a false light—at all events, in a light in which we ought no longer to regard Him. The Law is regarded as characterized by severity, fierceness, fire, terrors : and it is particularly noted that these features of sternness stand out in the account of the giving of the Law on Mount Sinai. Doubtless they do; and the contrast is noticed in the Epistle to the Hebrews between the severity of the Law and the tenderness of the Gospel. But we must take care not to exaggerate the contrast. The accessories, the circumstances, the manner of giving the Law, were calculated to strike terror—thunder and lightning, the crashing blast of the trumpet, the fire and smoke; but this outward exhibition of terribleness afforded no proof that He, Who so ordered it all, was a harsh relentless immoveable despot: even His terrors are modified by kindly consideration. GOD could not divest Himself of His own inherent awfulness and dazzling majesty, but He made His attributes as approachable as possible, through the provisions He laid down, that the people should not come too near, and by the mediation of Moses, who was to stand between Him and them. And in His words He shewed Himself a Father of mercies and GOD of Love.

The GOD of the Gospels is the GOD of Mount Sinai. The GOD Who utters blessings in the Sermon on the Mount is equally loving—brimming

with Love ineffable—though Sinai burned with
fire. Jehovah is 'the same yesterday, to-day,
and for ever,' revealing Himself to the lawgiver
and mediator Moses as 'the LORD merciful and
gracious.' *We* may change : He never does.
Our temper may alter our power of sight, may
blind, distort, our notions of His attributes.   Our
rebelliousness may make it necessary for Him to
shew rigour, to punish, threaten, strike awe : but
He is the same : His Name is still 'I AM :' He
is still Love.   If you doubt it, consider the text,
spoken to His servant Moses, of a people whom
He was bearing in His Everlasting Arms to a land
flowing with milk and honey—a people, notwithstanding these signal mercies, stubborn and
rebellious beyond belief.   It expresses His wish
that His people would so live that He might be
able to bless them.   As a Father, with affection
beyond that of any human father, any human
mother, He yearns over His children, watching
with intense interest their path, as they swayed
to and fro in alternate obedience and disobedience,
and expressing Himself to that holy man who
had caught something of the Divine Love himself
in longing for the salvation of His people—'O
that there were such an heart in them, ... that
they would keep My Commandments alway.' . . .
The most loving friend cannot wish more for
another than his best welfare in the best of
blessings.

Consider, (1) 'Fear Me, and keep My Commandments always.' These words, coming immediately after the recital of the Decalogue, contain a general allusion to the ten laws : and a question forthwith arises as to how far the Ten Commandments are binding on Christians.

On the principle that the Old and New Testaments are inseparable, and inspired by the same Spirit, we naturally conclude that there must be something in the Ten Commandments requisite for us to observe. Our Blessed Saviour, speaking of them in the Sermon on the Mount, says that He came not to destroy the Law but to fulfil it : and His comment on several of the Commandments is not to explain them away, or declare man's exemption from their observance, but rather to clench their obligation more firmly. And this He does by asserting a higher deeper law, which involves but exceeds those ancient laws ; His argument being, Not only are those laws binding, but you must go further. If the Sixth denounces murder, the Christian Expositor denounces anger : that is, the letter of that law binds, but the spirit of it also. The Ten Commandments are not worn out and antiquated ; they contain a moral element, a root of right action and right principle, which not only cannot be dispensed with, but must be enlarged upon. All contain a moral principle—love to GOD, love to man. The Fourth seems to be a ceremonial law, fixing a day for

14

worship, but involves a moral principle, *viz.* the duty of employing part of our time in devotion and worship : a definite period being fixed because the weakness of human nature requires fixed periods, lest 'any time' should become 'no time.'

But, as our LORD says, Christians must not content themselves with the observance of these Ten Commandments. Perfection must be our aim. Our love for man must be modeled after GOD'S Love, deep, catholic, unbounded : and our love for GOD must be reciprocal to His for us, an unrestrained overflowing gratitude, an unreserved devotion, an exhaustless loyalty. To keep His Commandments we must go to the root of them. It is not enough to sheathe the sword and not kill our neighbour—not enough to shun the very act of adultery—not enough to keep our hands from theft, our tongues from slander : but we must love our fellow-men and do them good, must be pure and chaste in all our thoughts, must give our neighbour his due, uphold his character, and wish him prosperity and success. We must not be niggards in our deeds of kindness, nor tied to the bare form and letter of charitable acts, but must foster a burning love for the souls and temporal welfare of all : not resting till we have done all in our power, both to honour GOD and benefit man.

(2.) 'O that there were such a heart in them, ... that it might be *well with them*.' Plainly then the keeping of GOD's Commandments ensures welfare. 'If thou wilt enter into life, keep the Commandments.' People talk of the burden and trouble of obeying GOD: it is tiresome (say they) and a thankless thing to be strict and religious. Those who do not try the pleasure of piety, of course will not understand that there can be any comfort in it. But there is more pleasure in serving GOD, than in any other course. I ask, Is it well with those who outrage GOD's laws? What sort of welfare is the happiness of the intemperate? I say nothing about the hourly misery which he or she brings on those living in the same house: but what happiness is it to *himself*? It is none, I am bold to say; unless, the breaking out of passions, the perpetual quarrels, the head-aches that follow, be pleasure; unless the reproofs of conscience (where she is not quite stifled) be pleasure. Ah! men may love the world, but the world will not satisfy the needs of their inner souls. To get wealth, to indulge our own whims, to gain our own ends at the expense of others, with the certainty of brewing quarrels, and stirring up strife, and possibly losing our gains while we are grasping them most tightly;—this is not to win happiness: you cannot call it happiness. But the fear of GOD does bring peace. 'Her ways are ways of pleasantness, and all her paths are peace.' There is an inward satisfaction, a consciousness of having done the right thing, which makes the heart glow with pleasure; not unfrequently (but not always) an outward blessing, in earthly advantages—quite as often as in the case of the unprincipled—but, what is more than all, there is the peace of looking onwards. The keeper of GOD's commands is not afraid to think that death is coming, judgment coming; not afraid to part with earth, because it will be to welcome Heaven. 'Great is the peace that they have who love Thy Law.' 'Blessèd is the man that feareth the LORD; he hath great delight in His Commandments.'

A step further. When the great plunge is made, and the soul finds itself in the world beyond, where silver and gold will not buy comforts, and intellect and sinews are powerless; there, in 'the life which knows no ending,' which the ungodly try hard to believe has no existence, and is only the foolish fabrication of clergymen and others who preach against indulgence in earthly comforts, because they do not care for them—there, when it is too late to change the mind, too late to sue for pardon, too late to start afresh on truer principles—there, will those who have feared GOD, and believed in His Word, and kept His Commandments, find to their joy that it is well with them: the treasures of *that* kingdom will be theirs: the honours of Heaven, the pleasures of spiritual enjoyment, will be their own, when nothing else can give pleasure nor relief.

(3.) But mark : 'keep My Commandments *always*.' Steadfast, continuous, patient, must our obedience be ; not hot and cold in the service of GOD ; not a week of church-going and a week of dissipation. What value is there in a subject who is loyal sometimes, and sometimes rebellious —sometimes a friend, a foe sometimes ? GOD offers peace only to those who are patient and enduring in their holiness. There is no security but in endurance ; for if we are satisfied with an ague-fit of piety, the death-summons may come when the fit is off us. Suppose you have prayed —for a week or two, and then lived prayerless ; why, your soul's life must droop :—suppose you receive the Holy Communion at Easter, and not again for a year :—suppose you do a kind action to-day, and to-morrow begin to treat those about you unkindly :—there is no promise of real happiness to such conduct. Piety consists in settled habits of love to GOD and man : and if your breath passes away at the moment when your evil spirit has the upper hand, What *then?* ——

(4.) Again : 'O that there were such an heart in them that they *would* keep . . . . .' Here we have a Divine assertion of man's free-will. It lies with ourselves to choose—to do or not to do the Will of GOD. He does not force us to be good, nor prevent us from being good. It is with us, as with Adam and Eve; we may eat or eat not. It is with us, as with the Israelites, to whom Moses said, 'I have set before you life and good, death and evil.' It is still, 'Why *will* ye die?' 'Ye *will* not come unto ME, that ye might have life.' 'Whosoever *will*, let him take of the water of life freely.'

I have met with persons who answered, when urged to amend their lives, 'What's the use of trying? I can do nothing: if GOD chooses He can call me, and then I shall not be able to resist: but till then, I am unable to stir hand or foot.'

Now I am not disputing for a moment GOD's absolute, unfettered, sovereignty. His Will is law: His election absolute. 'Without ME, ye can do nothing.' 'Therefore hath He mercy on whom He will have mercy, and whom He will He hardeneth.' All this is true; but still, on the other hand, the choice is before us; we *can* choose. If not, GOD mocks us, bidding us choose when we cannot choose!

It is not for me to reconcile or explain the apparent inconsistency—that we are elected by GOD, yet free to choose. The two things seem inconsistent: never mind; both are true; wait for a solution.

There is something in every heart, if honest enough to look at itself, which says, 'It rests with thee, with thyself, whether thou wilt serve GOD or not.' It is perfectly true, 'By grace ye are saved; and that not of yourselves, it is the gift of GOD:' yet St. Peter says, 'Grow in grace,' that is, enjoins growth; and therefore growth, somehow, is in our own power. We talk of our uncontrollable impulses : but self-control is in our own hands, and may be acquired by practice. You stand at a high window, or on the edge of a cliff, you look down, and an unaccountable impulse prompts you to jump down, to certain death, you know. ·Is it not at such a moment in your power to draw back? If you let the sensation linger, it takes a decided shape—you cannot say what may happen, you may jump down. But you can draw back at once. If you play with the temptation, you will soon find it stronger than your will; but not at first, for there is a promise of a way of escape from every temptation. In other words, you *can* resist : the aid of GOD, which rises above all false notions about fate, is guaranteed to you. What becomes of the favourite boast of the superiority of man to the animals, if you deprive us of our power of free-will? Man is then like a stone, which drops to the earth by an inevitable law, and has no will.

But, Brethren, remember that this free-will implies two things. First, nobility, in having the power of choice, having the power of judgment, the ability to balance good and evil. But secondly, a heavy responsibility. Our destiny for joy or for ruin lies in our own hands. Whether we are happy now and in Heaven, or wretched now and in hell, rests with ourselves. We cannot shift the responsibility, any more than the murderer, who has deliberately planned his revenge, can plead temporary insanity. If the Evil One were irresistible; if GOD's decrees were not in any wise affected by our conduct, (the case of Nineveh shews that they are,) then our responsibility would cease. But with the offer of infinite grace, none can say that he is guiltless if his soul be lost.

Hear, I beseech you, the loving tenderness of our Heavenly Father. 'Oh! that there were such an heart in them, that they would fear Me.' What He yearns for—what Christ died for—what the Holy Ghost groans unutterably for—let us not despise, nor forfeit. Heaven is ours, *if we will*: if not, we choose, we *choose*, Hell. 'Have I any pleasure in the death of him that dieth?' No, says reason: No, says our own heart: 'for GOD so loved the world, that He gave His only begotten Son, that whosoever believeth on Him should not perish, but have everlasting life.'

SERMON XXII.

CHRIST INTERCEDING.

HEBREWS, VII. 25.

He ever liveth to make intercession for us.

'LIFT up your heads, O ye gates, and be ye lift up, ye everlasting doors, and the King of Glory shall come in.'

There was joy in Heaven when the glorified Body of Jesus Christ passed through the portals of the eternal Kingdom : joy at the completion of Redemption : joy at the salvation of sinners : joy —for the heavenly beings know no jealousy—at the sight of mankind exalted in Christ to GOD's right hand.

And there was joy in the breasts of the disciples when they bent their steps back to Jerusalem after Christ's Ascension to wait in the Holy City for the promised Spirit. And why?

⁎⁎

Because the great consolatory truth was gradually dawning on their minds, that their loved LORD was not lost for ever—not dead to them ; though out of sight, not forgetting them—though in Heaven, not disconnected with earth.

We can bear to part with a dear friend, if we know that he is gone to do us some good, and therefore cannot forget us, because his object is to work for us ; and that we shall, by and by, see him again. It is astonishing how we may be supported through a long separation by this sort of confidence, this faith in the intentions, in the sincerity, in the loving usefulness, of the friend from whom we are separated.

Now we are parted from our dear LORD—for a time only, but still parted. It is good for us ; as all that GOD ordains is good for us ; good as a discipline, good on account of what He is engaged upon for us.

Good as a discipline. If He were here, living in presence among us, should we be the better for it ? Earth, with Him walking upon it, would be too dear : we should have thoughts of Him too mean to be true and profitable. Should we not incline too much to fondle and rest in His outward form—to sit motionless, like Mary, at His feet, drinking in delight with our eyes—to be cumbered, like Martha, with much serving, in order to do Him earthly honour and courtesy— to draw our sword passionately, like St. Peter, against His enemies—to call down fire from heaven in indignation, like St. James and St. John—to be dissatisfied, like St. Thomas, with any less proof of His Presence than the thrusting the hand into His side? These things may be good in their place; but there is peril, lest we make too much of them, and by them our thoughts be drawn aside from our proper and necessary work.

For there is something to be done. And absence from Him summons us back to our recollection, till we ask what He would have us do. If we always had Him outwardly at hand to refer to, there would be no occasion then to brace up our consciences and decide between right and wrong by the exercise of our own reflection and judgment; we should fling ourselves into the arms of our unerring Guide, and our spiritual strength would in a moment flicker and go out. Christ came to restore the soul to its nobler instincts, to make it love holiness and live for Heaven. Even Christ's Presence ever on earth would make earth too dear, and that Presence itself too much 'of the earth, earthy.' Many things good in themselves become perilous if over-indulged. We need healthiness even in pious habits, which will become morbid, if not pruned and restrained by temperance. The soul grows unstrung, if it is always being soothed by sacred music, or is always under the influence of exciting devotional

services.   There is (what most of us feel to be)
the drudgery of Christian works, which is a most
necessary and wholesome discipline; done against
the grain perhaps, but done on principle.   We
need study, laborious painstaking study in Holy
Scripture, not the pleasurable perusal of only the
more dainty and luscious passages : we must dig
deep to find sacred truth.   In our prayers we
must exert ourselves, and strenuously beat our
wings in irrepressible endeavours to fly up to
GOD.   In receiving the Holy Communion, we
must not be content with anything less than the
straining of heart and mind to realize the unseen
and absent Saviour, till He becomes verily and
indeed present to our soul.   It is good to look on
the Cross, but in looking on it we may think too
absorbingly of *it*, and not enough of Him Who is
exalted from it to Heaven, and not enough of the
Work which He finished on it, and the power
which it is to exercise on our soul and every day
life.   It is quite possible to overflow with tender
emotions towards Christ our Saviour, to gaze
with brimming eyes on the sad, holy, and loving
features of the Crucified One, and yet in an
instant to be turned by some distracting accident,
or trivial interruption, into a temper and behaviour
in which all that is noble in Christ, all that we
should have copied from Him, all that He wished
to make us, is utterly lost, and we shew ourselves
unchristian and earthly in our passions and wishes.

Better therefore is the discipline of separation from Him, which leaves us enough of His influence here on earth to make us pine to be like Him, in the hope of being with Him hereafter. It is expedient for us that He went away: partly, because had He remained our souls would have worshipped the ground on which He trod; partly, because on His Ascent He sent down the Gift of the Holy Ghost, to be with us an abiding Comforter, not in visible form, to fetter our affections to that, but in unseen power, to spiritualize and make them heavenly.

Again, it is good for us to be parted from the LORD, because of what He is doing in His separation from us.

Why is He ascended? What does He? 'He ever liveth to make intercession for us.' He sitteth at the right hand of GOD, our crowned Champion. The diadem of victory is on His brows, and not the crown of thorns: His purple robe is the mantle of unsullied righteousness, washed and whitened by His very life-blood: the reed is changed into the rod of power: all foes crouch beneath His feet: there are now none to mock Him, or lift a finger against Him; for the very Archangels bow before Him, exalted Son of Man: GOD has given Him the Name which is above every name.

Surely it is good for us that He is at the right hand of Power. He is our Treasurer, has purchased eternal redemption for us, and stores up for us everlasting joys. He is getting in readiness, for all who will receive Him, the peaceful mansions in His Father's House. And if we reach that blessed Home, He will Himself be all in all to us, our joy and exceeding great reward.

But His great work now is Intercession: and how is this so great a boon?

'No man cometh unto the Father but by Me.' But He interposes no hindrance. Some who have power are capricious in using it: many a man who can, will not, help. If Queen Eleanor had not exerted the influence which she possessed with Edward III., the burgesses of Calais would have been sacrificed. If Judge Jeffreys, of execrated fame, had willed it, he might have saved many a poor creature whom in his wicked barbarity he sent to the gallows. But, if we may mention His Name in the same breath, He Who is the only Door to mercy, stands wide open for all to enter: He stints not His endeavours, but for ever and for ever pleads His Sacrifice of Atonement before the throne of GOD. He is not one who, safe himself, forgets others: nor, because He rests from His labours, has He no sympathy for others that toil on.

And at the very centre of all forces, helps, graces, and comforts, He stands. He speaks to the Head of all Power. There is no higher height to climb to. He, our glorified Brother, is Face to Face with the eternal GOD; yea, Himself is GOD. His influence is unbounded, for He is the well-beloved Son of the Father, the Holy One and the Just, a perfect Sacrifice and propitiation. He knows the mind of GOD, He cannot plead and not be listened to.

Has it not already been proved? He prayed the Father, and He *sent* another Comforter, that He might abide with us for ever.

Oh! Brethren, is it not good for us, that He has ascended into Heaven? Is it not necessary to believe it? For He ever liveth to make intercession for us.

If Christ be for us, who can be against us? The Accuser of the brethren, our adversary the Devil, can make no indictment stand against the pleading of the ascended Saviour. He is on our side: He intercedes for us: and we, by virtue of our connection with Him, are drawn up to Him, and receive the benefits of His intercession. In the Face of the exalted Son, the Father sees us; for we are in the Son, and by His merits and goodness we may stand.

Some, under colour of humility, profess to think that this Intercessor is not enough; or rather, because He is so high, that therefore we must fear to go near Him. Nay, but He says, ' Come unto Me;' it is faithless distrust and ungrateful suspicion not to comply with His call. Our

LORD's office of Intercessor ought indeed to incite us to copy His Example as intercessors, and much good may be done by our pleading for each other: but there is but One Mediator between GOD and men, the Man Christ Jesus; and Holy Scripture is silent, significantly silent, as to any further necessity for our going to angels or saints, or fellow-men, in order to gather courage to approach the LORD Christ. Yet, while condemning, as our Church does, prayers to the departed saints, I am not discouraging human intercessions in this world. The benefit which may be done is incalculable. Would that we practised it more! Many is the sin which might be stopped in others, many the ill-feeling which might be checked in ourselves, many the blessing, the grace, which might be won, by intercessory prayer; if only we would try to pray for others, instead of talking about being unfit, and not good enough. If you love your friend, and care for him, and pray for him; however far from being perfect you are, you would do him good, and do yourself good: for it will do anybody good, to kneel down and pray for somebody else.

But what if our Blessed Saviour's Intercession is useless? Useless! How can it be? Indeed, indeed, it can. Never useless in itself, but ineffectual because men counteract it. Many is the good, which is marred by misconduct or folly or thoughtlessness. Many is the child, who learns good at school, but unlearns it at home. It is of little use for teachers to pour in wholesome truth into the minds of children, if it is poisoned by bad example in parents. Instead of parents working with the school-master, they often take part with their children in opposition to the teacher, and then schooling is worse than thrown away. A boy is taught at school to be straightforward, obedient, steady : but if he sees his father dishonest, intemperate, or disrespectful, the good teaching in most cases is so much waste of time.

And so may all the precious effects of our LORD's Mediation be countervailed by our stubborn resistance to the influence of the Holy Spirit. Oh ! listen to me, all who fight against GOD's laws ! Don't dream that Christ can save you—even He, powerful as He is—if you will not be saved. A mother was once pleading for her son ; and the offended person promised for her sake to overlook the fault, if the lad would own to it ; but he would not, and so he forfeited the proffered pardon.

Let Christ therefore plead with you too, by all that He has done for you—by His Agony, His Crucifixion, His Triumph, for you—that you would consent so to live that His Intercession may avail. Not one sinner but that Mediation will save, if the sinner will be saved. Not one sinner will be saved by that Mediation, unless he will be saved.

Oh! look to it that those Prayers of His may not be prayed in vain for you; but try to live so above the miserable pleasures and attractions of this world, that your heart may be with your ascended LORD.

But on the other hand, if we work with Him, and struggle up out of habits of sin towards Him —if we, like the poor chained eagle, flutter with strong pinions to break from our bondage—then, even though for the present we remain prisoners, we shall in time be set free, to dart aloft into the sky with a scream and cry of victory.

Oh! that unwearied, never discouraged, patient Voice of Intercession, which Jesus utters! Whatever you may be doing, the Voice still pleads— pleads, while you are doing your best to serve and love Him—pleads while you are indifferent to His exertions—pleads, while you are doggedly resisting all His offers. Did you ever think of it as you were going to do some unholy action? Did you ever give it a thought, as you drank the maddening glass of spirits, as you walked forth at night to some scene of foul sin, as you framed a lie, or cherished spite, that above, in the silence of Heaven, a Voice was ever and ever speaking in your behalf, that fresh grace might descend and check you, and that GOD would in mercy spare you?

It is indeed an amazing problem, that, when all these almighty forces are at work for our salvation, and every power is brought into play, short of compulsion, to win souls to right things, any *one* should be so blind and stubborn as to reject the offer: that when Heaven is offered, his mansion being prepared for each, eternal joy lies before us —man deliberately, and violently too, seizes on sin, his curse, and hugs it to his bosom, to swear eternal friendship to it.

Be it not so with us!

'If any man have ears to hear, let him hear.'

John and Charles Mozley, Printers, Derby.

Check Out More Titles From HardPress Classics Series In this collection we are offering thousands of classic and hard to find books. This series spans a vast array of subjects – so you are bound to find something of interest to enjoy reading and learning about.

Subjects:
Architecture
Art
Biography & Autobiography
Body, Mind &Spirit
Children & Young Adult
Dramas
Education
Fiction
History
Language Arts & Disciplines
Law
Literary Collections
Music
Poetry
Psychology
Science
…and many more.

Visit us at www.hardpress.net

CPSIA information can be obtained
at www.ICGtesting.com
Printed in the USA
BVHW041807220819
556561BV00022B/5325/P